Exchanges

reading Janice Galloway's fictions

edited by Linda Jackson

Edinburgh Review

EDITOR: Ronald Turnbull
ASSISTANT EDITOR: Karina Dent

22a Buccleuch Place
Edinburgh EH8 9LN

Tel: 0131 651 1415

edinburgh.review@ed.ac.uk
www.edinburghreview.org.uk

EDITORIAL BOARD: Cairns Craig, Kimberly Hutchings, A.L. Kennedy,
Andrew O'Hagan, Christopher Whyte

ADVISORY BOARD: Jimmy Clawson, Peter Cudmore,
Karina Dent, David Moses

PRODUCTION: Peter Cudmore

Exchanges: reading Janice Galloway's fictions ISBN 1 85933 213 7
© the contributors, 2004

Printed and bound in the UK by Antony Rowe Ltd.,
Bumper's Farm, Chippenham, Wiltshire

Published by the Centre for the History of Ideas in Scotland,
University of Edinburgh

Supported by

Contents

There is no one at the other side?
Protecting the selves in Galloway's writing

Linda Jackson

Janice Galloway is one of Scotland's finest writers, with a contemporary narrative voice that is undeniably feminine. This is serious and noteworthy given that the Scottish literary tradition has not been widely known for its feminine *or* female pedigree.

It is some fifteen years since Polygon first published *The Trick is to Keep Breathing*, announcing the arrival of this major new talent. She is now a celebrated name in ever widening literary circles, and has enriched the canon with a diversity of short fiction, poetry, a play, an opera libretto and two further novels. Published in seven languages, Galloway has been a tremendous inspiration to many new writers—male and female—and clearly a book of critical essays that focus exclusively on her work is long overdue.

One of the things that has struck me most forcibly while reading these essays and discussing her writing is a deep sense of duality, fragmentation and loss. This may be across the gender divide, or between reader and narrator, among fractured identities or found in the oscillation between objective and subjective frames of reference. There is also a perceived notion of conflict within and across selves in her work, where we see meaning and contact struggle for a place in a world of few precious returns. However, it is in these returns that Galloway's writing conveys a real potential for connectedness, however fleeting this may be.

When reading her writing, one is aware of a penetrating and relentless search for ways of understanding human interaction, for new and experimental ways of tracing the layers of complexity that inform our attempts to enact or, at least occasionally, touch upon the truth of feeling. In response perhaps to the perceived failure of attempts to communicate these feelings adequately, we find characters retreat from the fray, close down into an intense and driven interiority where the 'black eye' of a manipulative and rationalising self reruns and replays motivations, actions and outcomes.

In finding ways of escape from subjective thoughts into the objective world, Darragh O'Grady notes that Galloway's characters embark on a 'disappearance strategy', a post-modern escape into shopping, tourism, drug use and media consumption. O'Grady convincingly links this 'disappearance' to the acute alienation of *Scottish* identity and more particularly *female* Scottish identity. Alexis Logsdon also considers the 'withdrawal' of Joy in *The Trick is to Keep Breathing* as part of a survival strategy in her restricted social and economic situation. In this essay, we find also a challenging reconsideration of the 'gothic' in Galloway's work that, while acknowledging the psychological realm (the focus of much gothic criticism), concentrates primarily on the socio-political dimensions which inform and almost necessitate Joy Stone's distorted consciousness.

In a stark contrast of tone and interpretation, Sharon Norris suggests an imaginary meeting between Joy Stone and Bridget Jones to see if there are any exchanges possible between these two women of similar age and with arguably similar issues. In this provocative reading Norris questions the feminist credentials of the writers through their characters' involvements with men, mastication, magazines and madness. Ironic humour is pervasive in both novels and it is irony that allows Joy an escape or distancing from herself in context. The voice in the margin, Norris argues, is frequently humour offering a form of private control, a revisiting while stepping outside.

Josianne Paccaud-Huguet considers how it is the private voices of women (*and children*) that we are made to hear in the 'post-modernist zones' of Galloway's work. She argues that the language of the texts enacts the impossibility of smooth textual relationships that in turn may serve as an analogy for the 'unbridgeable fault-line in Galloway's representation of gender relations'. In her analysis of Galloway's metaphors, Paccaud-Huguet reads cracked walls, plaster and mirrors in female spaces as representing an ever-splitting, fragmented female consciousness. In this she further argues that Galloway's narrative structures go beyond the scope of a narrow 'feminist' reading: 'what is at stake here is the truth of *difference*—in gender, race, nationality (and) age'.

Willy Maley takes a very serious yet humorous swipe, in his essay, at the ways in which the place of men has had a repressive and containing effect on female potential. He concentrates on the way in which a narrow and *harrowing* misreading of her work by a *male* critic limits and contains more 'fruitful' and meaningful interpretations. In this way, a negative masculine sensibility that Galloway points to in her work is ironically replayed. An opportunity for 'bridging' between narrator and reader was clearly seriously missed in Douglas Gifford's reading of Janice Galloway's writing. In considering this, I am immediately drawn to the essay by Carolyn Masel who develops this idea that the narrating subject or centre of consciousness is *feminine* and it is this that invokes one's own gender politics and response to the text.

Masel closely analyses Galloway's capacity and strategy for eliciting an empathetic response in her readers, a 'connection' that leaves both the reader and the narrator experiencing what Masel describes as a 'double take'. The relational element between the 'I' and the 'you' is explored and this may offer reassurance of connectedness across and between selves, but in the final analysis the protagonist's experience of doubling, the 'I' and 'you', seems more something that has to be endured rather than celebrated:

I am outside myself, watching from the corner of the room.

Ailsa Crum listens from *her* room to the haunting voice of Suzanne Vega as she reflects on Galloway's latest novel. Vega sings of an 'eloquent' silence; however in her reading of *Clara,* Crum talks about the repressive silencing of Clara Schumann who struggles to live under the tyranny of her father and the dependency of her husband. Her psychological strategies for survival seem to involve a distancing, a withdrawal into silence, inner debate and *domesticity* in order to 'get by'.

Galloway's fiction has been described as showing women trapped into passivity yet attempting to resist being silenced by conventional views of what they should be or do. It is however the case that many of the female protagonists in her work do continue to play the game. It is only through the channel of the interiorising narrator—whose sense of the real events taking place we must trust—that we have access to a sense that their feelings differ radically from their actions.

In *Clara* we read of her preparations for performance: to deny fear, exercise control and evoke emotion through containment. All of these come into play, not only when performing but when trying to live a life in love with Robert Schumann and his crippling manic depression. The intellectualising of Galloway's female characters and the distance that they need to maintain from freefall contact is as marked as their need to actually make this leap of faith. We read of Clara's 'terrible sensation of separateness that would not go away'. And yet engagement with the other is described as painful in this text as women's loving becomes a protective nurturing that must be carried to extremes for the love needed by Robert Schumann.

Ellen-Raïssa Jackson's 'Love in a Changing Environment' explores how Galloway's texts suggest the importance of place and its relation to identity. She further points to the reactive basis of everyday lives in Galloway's work and suggests that experiences are closely shaped by the immediate environment that the characters find themselves exposed to. Much of this essay looks at the stories in *Where You Find It*, a book that considers the possibilities of love against an oncoming tide of difference. Reviewers have criticised the negative portrayal of romantic love in these stories but in reading them one can detect a desperate attempt to shine light on some of the problems that hinder development within love relations. In trying to find solutions however, the narrative offers an ironic and often humorous insight into the probability and possibility of 'bridging the gap'. Attempts at connection in love are often found hopelessly wanting. The female characters are shown flagging up the pitfalls as the men retreat from identification of them. In the opening story, 'Valentine', Stella prepares heart-shaped sandwiches (for his piece-box) as a surprise for her partner. The narrator doesn't fail to highlight the gaping chasm between intention and result as the man opens these in the factory.

Colin Clark describes the males in Galloway's fiction as 'children of a larger growth', men who are unable to express emotion but retain control by assuming authority, employing a cold silence or spitting abuse. Clark suggests also that the males in the shorter fiction avoid culpability and seek out ways that prove or argue their freedom from blame. Women harbour the guilt.

Eve Lazovitz looks at self-destructive behaviour in women and reads it as a response to their feelings of guilt. This guilt is born from an awareness that female concerns are not acknowledged as important to society, guilt that if *she* attempts to 'grow' in these areas which feel important to her then someone else's growth will somehow be impeded. Joy Stone feels guilt for feeling too much, for feeling too intensely in a society dominated by repression. Lazovitz uses water imagery, reading Joy as an 'island, separated from others by obscure waters... unable to swim'.

In reviewing her first poetry collection, *Boy, Book, See* Adam Piette finds Galloway trace the paths of water, memory and childhood. The collection harbours an acute tracing of detail, a *homing* in on concentrated topics. In Galloway's treatment of water, Piette notes that the collection bridges a culture of contamination and the contamination of culture.

This is serious.

In a culture that is repressive, the truth of feeling is contaminated by fear. Throughout Galloway's work, there are poignant glimpses of connection but also an acute recognition of separateness. In the finishing piece from *Where You Find It,* Galloway examines the acceptance of loss. 'Six Horses' brilliantly describes the aching at the end of a love affair:

> There is no one at the other side. She'd rather go home tonight, she says. Tonight she won't stay. Cab and a train, he says. This is serious. (p. 218)

Love, class, the self, the nation, the children: Galloway's themes are wide-reaching, her narrative style wide-arching.

In trying to 'come off the page', Galloway's method endeavours to remove (or suspend) the fundamental barrier between reader and text.

Perhaps her interiorising narrators represent many women who find themselves playing the game (or not) while waiting to see if there is indeed anyone at the other side.

We are reading *and listening to* the silences in her musical texts.

Love in a changing environment
Placing Janice Galloway's short stories

Ellen-Raïssa Jackson

In a review of Janice Galloway's second collection of short stories, *Where you find it*, Maggie Gee describes Galloway as a 'poet of uneasy intimacies in small spaces'.[1] Indeed, much of Galloway's short prose does read like poetry, perhaps because the meticulous recreation of the smallest everyday acts exposes so dramatically the gaps in the logic of living. So much is unsaid, or half articulated, that the objects which surround us take on some of the burden of living for us. It is a poetry of place, where ideas and emotions can only be apprehended through the environment in which they are mediated; Galloway is asking us to look carefully at the smallness of life, to see where we are.

In this respect her writing resembles the stories of James Kelman. Here the fascination with detail is part of an attempt to remove the mysterious authority of the writer, the dictatorial tyranny of narrative. Kelman's experiments in this field have been much discussed (see for example Cairns Craig, 'Resisting Arrest' and Kelman's own 'The Importance of Glasgow in my Work'), particularly his desire to undo the hierarchy of dialogue and narrative that consigns regional working-class figures to the margins of literature, extras in the screenplay of language. Kelman's work not only

---

1.   Maggie Gee, 'From the Edge of the Everyday'. *Times Literary Supplement*, 3 May 1996.

succeeds in breaking down this crippling distinction between inner and outer speech, between abstraction and articulation, but also overcomes a fundamental barrier between reader and text. Thus Kelman's painstaking catalogue of tiny details overwhelms the reader with the experience of poverty or unemployment; the comforting voice of the narrator is no longer there to relieve the intensity of the description, there is no voice of authority to tempt the reader into judgement or to allow her the fantasy of objective experience.[2] Similarly, Galloway's use of voice and perspective attacks entrenched literary practice through continually re-centring the experience of the margins, and by locating the particular and the vital (in all senses) in the ordinary.

Yet Galloway displays a broader concept of the dynamics of people and place than Kelman, a more pressing sense of the possibility that folk may not fit their own lives. She does this partly through a use of uncompromising humour; her characters often (although not always) sense the irony and alienation implicit in their preoccupations. This is not laughter as band-aid, nor as proof of humanity (as is sometimes the case in Kelman) but as the mocking of any form of self-regard, including the self-regarding pose of literary fictions. Whereas Kelman's refusal to use a single standard narrative voice can be extremely liberating on one level, on another it immerses the characters (and readers) so fully in their own text that all possible incongruity, even difficulty, seems to disappear. Galloway's handling of distance even within a first person narrative is a strong counter to this, and her sharp humour bursts the bubble of individual sovereignty. This deflation removes the comfort of familiarity and thus prevents any straightforward inversion of power relations, undercutting the binary models of political struggle. Galloway makes us aware of this kind of space as a meeting point for ways of seeing and ways of being, pulling out all the contradictions between individual and social identity. In this chapter I will discuss Galloway's treatment of place and the issues of shaping and belonging which her writing addresses. I will go on to consider how this relates to national identity, and the role of Scottish literature in defining the space of Scottish identity. Finally, I hope to show how Galloway's approach to place demonstrates her commitment to an ongoing relationship between art, nation and experience.

---

2.   Cairns Craig, 'Resisting Arrest: James Kelman', in Gavin Wallace and Randall Stevenson (eds.), *The Scottish Novel Since the Seventies: New Visions, Old Dreams* (Edinburgh: EUP, 1993); James Kelman, *Some Recent Attacks: Essays Cultural & Political* (Stirling: AK Press, 1992); James Kelman, *Not Not While the Giro and Other Stories* (Edinburgh: Polygon, 1983).

A key text in the consideration of these different aspects of Galloway's work is 'Love in a changing environment' from her first collection, *Blood*.[3] In this story a couple move into a flat above a baker's shop and find their life dictated by the smell of warm yeast and 'the sweet fat reek of doughnuts' (p. 17). Their relationship mirrors the patterns of the commodities sold downstairs, so that when the bakery is turned into a butcher's the warmth of lovemaking is replaced by violent suspicion—distrust accompanied by the 'the cracking of bone, the drill and the saw' (p. 19). Finally the arrival of a bone grinder proves too much and the narrator leaves both flat and lover.

The rhythm of the baker's shop is both external and intrinsic to the lovers' relationship. The opening sentence, 'The bakery was how we found it' (p. 17), is easily missed, yet crucial in this respect because it shows that while the lives of the lovers are pervaded by their immediate environment, that environment remains impervious to them.[4] Although the bakery closes down, it is not as a direct result of any action by the couple upstairs; indeed they seem to be one of its best customers. The couple take their cues from their environment; having only 'one room and no clock' they are totally dependent upon the different products baked throughout the day: 'hours shifted on white toasters and morning rye to mid-morning Eccles cakes and iced Chelsea rounds' (p. 17). This dependency extends to their diet and lovemaking, so that when the bakery sells up they are reduced to 'toastless beans and cheddar at teatime' or baked potato carry-outs which become a source of guilt and acrimony—'he quibbled with my choice of fillings'. The bakery is more than a background to their lives, it is a living context which plays an active role in them, pervading and defining even their thoughts, so that 'the surrounding air was everything and sweet' (p. 18).

The rather obvious connections between sense and sensuality become far more interesting when Galloway links them with phrases such as 'the animal vapour of cream meringues' (p. 17) or 'the flaccid thud of something thick splaying out against wood' (p. 19); it is precisely these kind of compressed images that invite comparison to poetry. Bread as a symbol of love and indulgence and butcher's meat as one of violence and separation is compounded by the invasiveness of the ambience; this is not simply an imaginative use of standard literary devices (such as transferred epithets or

---

3. Janice Galloway, *Blood* (London: Minerva, 1992). Subsequent page numbers refer to this edition.
4. This sentence also pre-empts the title of the collection, *Where you find it*, thus linking it to a whole series of ambiguous experiences of love.

anthropomorphism). Rather, it is a linguistic exploration of the interlocking patterns of experience and the reactive basis of everyday life. The humour in this story depends upon those clichés of romantic narrative—'all-consuming passion', 'tell-tale signs of an affair'—which have become so familiar through popular romance novels, film and TV soaps, but whose location in a fresh context produces images of heightened irony. Thus the lipstick-on-the-collar motif of unfaithfulness becomes an illicit encounter with baking: 'Sometimes he went out without saying where he was going, coming home with crumbs on his lapel' (p. 19). Similarly the narrator reacts to the bakery's closure and its ominous implications for the relationship with pulp fiction sentiment: 'an iced finger ran the length of my spine but I pushed it away' (p. 18).

The allusions to a vocabulary of melodrama in 'Love in a changing environment' are not simply humorous, but also point the reader to the weakness of the narrator and the relationship. Although the couple look for growth, just as they tenderly water their African violet in the hope that 'there would be flowers' (p. 18), they lack the self-definition which would allow them to achieve such a flowering. Instead they rely on the self-raising flour of the shop downstairs and the received language of romance. Their own experiences and emotions are displaced and comprehensively replaced by the environment. Even the narrator's quasi-moral at the end of the story can be seen as a maxim of self-denial (again a reaction, rather than radical change or active intervention), the banal content of which works directly against its tone. Like the new flat which smells 'only of damp', the narrator's attitude is suspiciously wet: 'Thinner and wiser, I eat no meat and avoid cakes. The very sight of them makes me sick' (p. 19). There is no suggestion here that the narrator has rejected the influence of self-definition. The closing sentence remains firmly within the same defensive frame of reference that both characterised and condemned the relationship earlier in the story.

Although 'Love in a changing environment' is not set explicitly in Scotland, we can compare the struggle between the discourses of place and identity to the colonial relationship of Scotland and England. Scotland as a country is at once a part of Britain and a separate entity; the glibness that frequently subsumes Scotland within a homogenous Britain or even an all-encompassing England has as its counterpart a reactive, defensive and negative assertion of its identity as non-English or anti-English. Like the lovers, it has no original input into the dynamic of self-definition. Scottish difference emerges as denial, rather than affirmation: something that is subject to the changing milieu, and yet trapped in a fixed discursive space.

Indeed 'Love in a changing environment' could be said to enact a certain division between those supposedly timeless and most marketable aspects of Scotland: the sweetness of shortbread versus the butchery of *Braveheart*. The lack of resources, linguistic or otherwise, that this implies is an argument in itself for Scottish writing, not simply as 'resistance', but as self-articulation and the creation of other, overlapping and adaptable narratives.

Life in a changing environment is the topic of much of Galloway's work. Ideas about the importance of place and its relation to identity are constantly developed and revisited, from the 'Scenes from a Life' stories and 'Plastering the Cracks' in *Blood* to stories like 'a night in' and 'tourists from the south arrive in the independent state' in *Where you find it*.[5] 'A night in' is comparable in length to 'Love in a changing environment' and shares the latter's concern with the mutual relationship between people and place. In this story, the place in question is a half-finished house on a building site where a couple (Stevie and an unnamed narrator) come looking for shelter on a stormy night. Like the bakery, the half-built house has a living presence, but also a more subtle relationship with its inhabitants.

The house is full of the discarded objects of the workmen who are building it, 'an empty beer can, cigarette cartons, rags of newspaper' (p. 39), shadows of animals and insects and the couple themselves, huddled inside a single coat. In this case the relationship between the structure of what will be a house and all the life that has passed through it becomes reciprocal: the 'skeleton of the building' is an open, living entity which whines 'like someone asleep, wrestling with dreams' (p. 40) and of which they become a part. For the narrator this recognition is a privilege: 'we were seeing something intimate, something the people whose home this would become would never see or even think about' (p. 40). She goes on to describe the various transient visitors—cats, birds, people, insects—as 'pitted into the unplastered brick', a material part, if secret and secreted, of this home-to-be. The structure of the building provides shelter, but is itself made up of spaces and absences, 'holes in every wall', the footprints of departed workmen and the aspirations of future residents. The space which will be a house constitutes a blueprint for a continuous community in which the final inhabitants' awareness of the traces of other, earlier occupants is less important than their material connection.

The spaces of the house are invitations both to movement and rest. They

---

5. Janice Galloway, *Where You Find It* (London: Jonathan Cape, 1996). All subsequent page references are to this edition.

draw the reader's attention to the indeterminacy of the distinctions between inside and outside; the windows are not yet 'shut up with glass' but are holes which let in light, rain and thunder. The floors are not in place and the narrator's eye is drawn by the flame of a match upwards to the 'vertiginous height of the scaffolding' (p. 40). These descriptions, together with the coming and going of workmen and animals, prevent the story from settling too comfortably into place. At the same time the focus of the story moves from outside the house, into a room, to one of its corners and finally to Stevie's open coat. This movement inwards is encapsulated in one particular moment where a flash of lightning gives the narrator 'a single snapshot of this place that would be a room, Stevie in one of its corners, waiting for me' (p. 41). The invitation, both of Stevie's open coat and the house itself is one of togetherness, rather than isolation. Yet the sense of community is undermined by its transience; the continuity hinted at earlier in the story becomes more ambivalent as we consider the scene as a 'snapshot', an instant. The couple are presumably homeless, and their displacement contrasts sharply with the strong direction of the story's narrative. The dreamlike quality of the couple's visit emphasises this ambivalence towards the stop-gap sense of belonging; they are not at rest, but 'waiting for thunder' (p. 41). This raises the questions surrounding physical and metaphorical homelessness and their relation to the sense of longing and belonging explicit in any idea of national identity. These ideas are developed in a number of Galloway's stories and this is a point to which I shall return.

In her short stories, Galloway often looks to Scotland as a more expansive context for the spaces in people's lives on which she focuses. This appeal to the nation is highly productive because it brings with it the whole question of Scotland's unresolved political status. 'Scottishness' is perhaps best represented by the gaps in the fictions of the 'United' Kingdom and those markers of Scotland—tartan, whisky, bagpipes, Irn Bru. The lack of fit between the social identity offered by such symbols and the individual experience explored in the stories is not particularly surprising. What is compelling is the way that Galloway uses this disparity to challenge a certain type of identity politics.[6] This kind of politics relies on what Lawrence

---

6. These ideas have of course been discussed at great length in Scotland. See particularly Tom Nairn's description of the 'tartan monster' in *The Break-up of Britain* (London: Verso, 1983); Colin McArthur (ed.), *Scotch Reels: Scotland in Cinema and Television* (London: BFI Publishing, 1982); and for a response to these, Craig Beveridge and Ronald Turnbull, *The Eclipse of Scottish Culture: Inferiorism and the Intellectuals* (Edinburgh: Polygon, 1989).

Grossberg calls a 'synecdochical' model of identity: where the part (the individual) stands for the whole (the nation), and then goes on to expose the whole as unrepresentative and finally non-identical.[7] The casualty of this model is community, because its conclusion must inevitably be that the individuals in a group have different experiences or concerns and therefore the group is insignificant, incoherent or simply doesn't exist. To some extent this is a static model of identity that fails to recognise the process of identification as a form of movement, a coming together. This is where the Scotland of Galloway's stories is most intriguing: more than a gap of recognition, this Scotland is continually re-presented through different viewpoints, registers and typographies.

Galloway challenges this model of identity by highlighting the imbalance of power in the act of representation, specifically by refusing male dominated prescriptions of Scottishness that distort and confine the space of national identity. Marilyn Reizbaum, when speaking of another prominent female Scottish writer (Liz Lochhead) says:

> What she sees in the reductive presentation of her culture by the British and even the Scottish media is the historical interaction between the marginalization of culture and sexism.[8]

In 'Fearless', Galloway attacks 'the hard volatile maleness of the whole West Coast Legend' which feeds on its own image and protects itself with notions of loyalty and tradition. The eponymous male figure, whose targets are women and children, is tolerated and even defended through a certain 'respect' for that Legend:

> …some people seemed to admire this drunken wee tragedy as a local hero. They called him *a character*, […] You felt that it would have been shameful, disloyal even, to admit you hated and feared it. So you kept quiet and turned your eyes away.[9]

---

7. Lawrence Grossberg, 'The space of culture, the power of space', in *The Post-Colonial Question: Common Skies, Divided Horizons,* Ian Chambers and Lidia Curti (eds.), (London: Routledge, 1996), pp. 169–188.
8. Marilyn Reizbaum, 'Canonical Double Cross: Scottish and Irish Women's Writing', in Karen R. Lawrence (ed.) *Decolonizing Tradition: New Views of Twentieth-Century 'British' Literary Canons* (Chicago: University of Illinois Press, 1992), p. 182.
9. 'Fearless', in *Blood,* p. 113.

Galloway suggests that the male refusal to acknowledge the damage that Fearless does to his chosen victims is related to 'the general problems of being a colonised nation'.[10] This is part of a comprehensive rejection of a single, unitary identity which presents nationality and gender as conflicting demands. Instead her constantly shifting narrative voice explicitly recognises the difference from itself by its conflicting perspectives, particularly when it rests with women and children.

The tension between movement and stasis in 'a night in' is a form of literary counterpoint that can be compared to Galloway's experiments with perspective in her earlier stories. In *Blood*, an overtly manipulated viewpoint and 'camera angles' are frequently used to increase the importance of space and location. 'The Community and the Senior Citizen' is a good example of the effectiveness of these techniques. The story begins with a health visitor drinking tea at the home of a frail and elderly woman. After the health visitor's 'professional and crafted leave-taking', the woman prepares a leave-taking of her own, taking an overdose of pills and lying down to await death.

The narrative opens with a description which falls somewhere between a movie pitch and the passage which sets the scene at the beginning of a play. Similarly, the dialogue is set out as if it were a film or play script, with the names of the characters in capitals, and their actions indicated by the use of italics. The focus on the room is self-consciously adjusted to fit the action, so 'we can afford a little sentimental soft-focus' when the 'OLD WOMAN' appears and our gaze is then directed as if following her movements, shut out from the action when she closes doors, guided from a view of the whole room to the examination of a single object. Later in the story, the old woman mimics this scene-setting by re-organising the furniture and arranging the 'props' needed to take an overdose. The significance of her actions is continually undercut by the foregrounding of its observation. When she does take the pills the narrator comments: 'It takes about four minutes in all, not a long performance, and manages to retain interest throughout' (p. 57). The effect of this studied positioning is astonishingly disconcerting, because it moves the subject of the story away from the woman on to the reader and thus visits upon us those issues of community and responsibility with which the story deals as well as those inherent in reading itself. The alienation effect is comparable to that achieved by the intense scrutiny of everyday occurrences

10. She refers to this in the context of literature in her introduction to *Meantime: Looking Forward to the Millennium,* Women 2000 (Edinburgh: Polygon, 1991), p. 6.

that I mentioned earlier; the weekly invasion by the health visitor is at best a poor substitute for emotional support, and at worst a particularly heartless form of surveillance. Similarly, Galloway invokes the politics of reading as a demonstration of participation: there is no camera angle, no narratorial stance that is non-political because the space of observation can never be objective, it is always involved.

In *Where you find it* Galloway largely abandons the cinematic technique in favour of a shifting narratorial voice, often achieved through a marked absence of pronouns or by the juxtaposition of two stories from opposite standpoints; 'babysitting', for example, is told from the point of view of a little boy, and is followed by 'someone had to', a self-justifying account of a man who abuses his step-daughter. The voice of these stories moves easily between class, gender and sexual preference, breaking down what Homi Bhabha calls the 'social totalities' which are produced by the tendency of narrative authority to provoke 'a continual slippage into analogous, even metonymic categories, like the people or "cultural difference" that continually overlap in the act of writing'.[11] Bhabha is talking specifically here of the 'ambivalence of the nation as narrative strategy' and, as I suggested earlier, Galloway's technique is directed towards the creation of an anti-essentialist notion of Scottishness that is open to the different experiences of age, class and gender, whilst at the same time recognising common commitments and shared concerns. This approach to 'Scottishness' can be compared to bell hooks' description of black identity as 'yearning', a delicate balance of longing and belonging.[12] In hooks' analysis of the significance of post-modern thought for contemporary black experience she characterises radical subjectivity as a search for 'fertile ground for the construction of empathy'. This desire for a sense of groundlessness calls for 'ways to construct self and identity that are oppositional and liberatory … without privileging some voices by denying voice to others'.[13] In Galloway's work, this conflict between the need for a meaningful sense of concepts such as Scottishness and community, without imposing a pre-existing narrative of 'authentic' experience, is strongly related to the argument for a non-reactive Scottish

---

11. Homi K. Bhabha, *Nation and Narration*, (London: Routledge, 1990), p.6 and p.292. See especially pp.291–322.
12. See bell hooks: 'Postmodern Blackness' in Patrick Williams and Laura Chrisman (eds.), *Postcolonial Discourse and Postcolonial Theory: A Reader* (Hemel Hempstead: Harvester, 1994), pp.421–7.
13. ibid. p.425.

literature. There can be no objective view of Scotland, no absolute marker of Scottish identity, since these are all part of the ongoing encounter with Scottishness. In this respect, all Scottish writing is involved in the political issue of Scotland's status as a nation. No matter how specifically Scottish or otherwise its subject matter, such writing enacts the continuity of articulation which allows us a sense of community.

A particularly interesting story in this respect is 'the bridge', one of the few pieces in *Where you find it* overtly concerned with the complex relationship between art, nation and experience. 'the bridge' is about attempts to reach people, primarily Fiona's attempts to reach out to Charlie, but it is also about the role of art and whether it can or should connect people. In the story, Fiona is visiting Charlie in London. Both are painters from Scotland, but whilst for Charlie 'a place is just a place', Fiona is less sure that London provides an escape from the narrow-mindedness that Charlie despises in Scotland. The couple walk along the river towards a bridge where Fiona almost trips over a homeless man to whom she tries to give some money. As she looks for the purse she realises that she has met this man on an earlier occasion, when she handed him a few coppers and he gave her a sarcastic kiss in return. This time, Fiona has no change and hastily drops a twenty pound note in a box on which is written 'I NEED MONEY', before running to the bridge to catch up with Charlie. They stand on the bridge together and discuss '*being Scottish*' and the relationship between Life and Art. Fiona is looking for 'some kind of possibility opening up between them', but Charlie seems oblivious to her need for contact and refuses to kiss her as they turn to go home. They leave the bridge, where there is no longer any sign of the homeless man, and return home in silence.

Early in the story Fiona stresses the importance of self-location, an awareness of context. She describes her sense of belonging to Glasgow, half flippantly, as 'the only place I know how to work the buses' (p. 146), but also recognises it as a 'kind of … relief'. Charlie, on the other hand, interprets this attitude as a refusal to move outside known experience: 'scared of the big bad world out there. Some folk are uncomfortable anywhere but in a rut' (p. 148). Whilst Fiona feels a certain desire to be 'sophisticated or cosmopolitan', she is anxious to break down such a value-laden opposition between the two cities: 'London isn't the Big World at all … It's also as parochial as get out' (p. 149). Fiona's conflicting emotions, that is to say her suspicion of 'the establishment' and her commitment to the community ('being Scottish'), are mocked by Charlie as being those of an 'Unreconstructed Romantic' and this is backed up by her excuses for Charlie's behaviour—'artistic volatility' (p.146)—and her recognition of her own desire for 'something as trivial as a compliment' (p.153). In contrast, Charlie rejects 'Scottish culture jesus christ' and is apparently uninterested in any sense of community: 'I don't think I want to belong to anything. Except art maybe' (p.148).

However, Galloway is careful not to give authority to either the 'art for art's sake' argument, nor credence to the cult of the impoverished artist rising above experience. Charlie never asks Fiona about her work, yet still claims to know 'where women always fuck up' (p.153), by prioritising 'two kids and the glory of motherhood' over 'making a name for [themselves]', and he dismisses this as 'sentimentality'. Galloway deliberately maintains our sympathy for Fiona by exposing Charlie's vision of art and experience as equally romantic in its own way. Charlie claims to see too much—'See, my trouble, Fiona, my trouble is I'm too observant. I *see* everything. If I didn't order some of it on canvas, I'd go round the bend' (p.151). Yet this image of the tortured artist is shattered when they leave the bridge and the man lying in the scrub has disappeared and 'Charlie didn't seem to notice' (p.154). Similarly, Charlie fails to see that Fiona actively participates in the Scottish culture which he so readily dismisses, both by 'working the buses' and by 'her own pictures' (p.148). Indeed, Charlie seems not to notice much at all: from Fiona's presence as he paints, to the man by the bridge, he sees little. The narrative exposes this blindness as a form of self-regard that relies as much on a pre-existing stereotype as does Fiona's vision of Art and Life.

The homeless man whom Fiona encounters at the foot of the bridge is more central to the story than he at first seems. The homeless are not simply symbols of displacement in Galloway's stories, nor are they there to induce guilt in middle-class readers (although they might well do both of these things). The homeless man, like the couple in 'a night in', is a concrete reminder of that disparity between life and art. The words on the cardboard box in front of him are more of a statement than an appeal: 'I NEED MONEY' is a way of telling it like it is without worrying about the aesthetics of the act itself. By reading the box, Fiona is no longer innocent, she has recognised that need, and as she reflected earlier: 'you didn't start things you couldn't finish, create expectations and just fuck off' (p.141). In her previous encounter with this man we discover that we cannot know people by their circumstances, environment or what Charlie calls their 'priorities'. The homeless man uses 'English public school vowels', has beautiful hands, 'soft and plump beneath the dirt', and 'a straight stare' (p.144). The man's attitude is not deferential, not reducible to that of a vagrant alcoholic or psychiatric patient, rather he is shown to be every bit as 'ordinary' as Charlie. In direct contrast to Charlie, the first time he approaches Fiona he kisses her—a sarcastic response to pennies she gives his open hand. The kiss is a bridge between the two, an acknowledgement of the man's need and existence. Charlie's failure either to kiss Fiona or to see this man at all undermines his position as the voice of Art. His viewpoint presumes the authority of art over experience, an authority that fails to examine its own presumptions.

Homelessness in Scotland is the 'Big Issue' as the title of the magazine suggests.[14] Every year around eighty thousand Scots become homeless and each night more than one thousand people sleep rough in Scotland. This is an issue which cuts across borders, with substantial numbers of Scottish people migrating to London, looking for work and sleeping rough.[15] The homeless as encountered in literature are all too often characterised as 'drunken Scots' or incoherent tramps with strong regional accents. Their presence in the metropolis demonstrates the huge gaps in income and expectations produced by modern post-industrial life. This is a problem in many countries across the world, but one which is all the more acute for cultures where there is a high experience of emigration: this is the double-squeeze of Scotland's relationship with empire. Yet Galloway is well aware that individual identity cannot function as unproblematically representative of national identity. The man is English precisely because he cannot enact the lack of home on a wider scale. This puts the nationalist urge towards self-determination in perspective and at the same time re-emphasises the need for a stronger sense of communal responsibility, an imaginative space that can be called home in order to provide a physical one.

The antithesis of the homeless figure in these stories is the tourist, a privileged visitor, and a consumer of culture rather than its creator. Galloway parodies the juxtaposition of the imagined space of Scotland with the physical one in 'tourists from the south'. Scotland is defamiliarised by vocabulary that links it with the so-called 'second world' of Eastern Europe or 'the Eastern Bloc'. Scottish-English relations are characterised as those of a north/south divide that has been through a 'Cold War' but has now gone 'the way of the modern world … forging proud independences' (p. 159). The story is told

---

14. *The Big Issue* is the title of a magazine sold by homeless people in the UK (its counterpart in Ireland is called *The Big Issues*). The vendor receives 60% of the cover price of every copy sold.
15. Figures from Shelter report, *Housing for Good* (1995).

from the point of view of the tourists themselves, brimming with expectations prompted by their only other experience of Scotland: 'TV documentaries, the odd series. *Taggart, Para Handy*' (p. 160). Aside from the references to Eastern Europe these descriptions also draw on the narrative of empire—intrepid explorers dealing with difficult natives, together with a whole series of related ideas such as 'colonisation as civilization' and 'natives as children'. The tone of the story is one of great patience: 'odd that their countries being formally separate now should make them feel so much closer, so much more tolerant' (p. 159). The irony here is the suggestion that it is the 'Islanders' as opposed to the tourists who are 'tolerant', in that they largely ignore them.

The various clichés of Scottish culture are presented together to expose the expectations of the tourists. On the bus they take from the airport to the hotel, for example:

> The seats were pleasingly whole and covered with tartan flocking despite the strong tang of nicotine and spilled alcohol. Still everything seemed very clean. They were sure it was all very clean. (p. 161).

Galloway draws attention to the difference between representation and experience here as a demonstration of the obvious problems of national identity. No representation can ever be fully comprehensive, because like the synecdochical model of identity it is a part standing for the whole. The tourists' dismay, 'fifteen floors high in the New Independence Hotel ... that things were not all they had hoped for' is not simply due to a lack of fit between the packaged culture ('THE BEAUTIES OF ROYAL DEESIDE') and the one they are presented with, but also to the fact that all those different markers of Scotland, (such as alcohol, tartan, nicotine, bagpipes and expletives) are found in the same place. The realisation that Black Watch shagpile maketh not a nation isn't much of a revelation, but Galloway obliquely suggests that all representation, and specifically national representation, cannot simply be consumed—it demands a certain engagement. 'The Kelman novels they had brought for atmosphere would wait or be used, spines cracked open, to place over weary faces to keep out the morning light' (p. 163): whether they are read or not, the Kelman novels function as a barrier between the 'tourists' and 'the independent state'. Galloway less than subtly suggests that the fault lies with the tourists who value Kelman's writing for its 'atmosphere' rather than its content, and whose attitude is fundamentally patronising: 'they thought how understanding they had wanted to be. How generous. How tolerant. How kind.' (p.164)

This story is neither atmospheric, tolerant, nor kind. However it is more than a little generous when it comes to consider its own understanding in contrast with that of the tourists. It is one of Galloway's less satisfying stories, perhaps because it approaches its subject too directly. Like Fiona's attack on 'the establishment' in 'the bridge' it fails to recognise its own place in the critique; it becomes as reductive as those representations of Scotland which rely on a single set of symbols—be they those of *Para Handy* or of *Taggart*. The weakness of the story can also be related to the lack of engagement in the narrative, although as part of a broader project which contrasts directly with the perspective of the 'the bridge' it is much more successful. There are many 'tourists' in Galloway's writing and this story shows the tourist-as-tourist, in 'The Community and the Senior Citizen', for example.[16] The absolute separation implied in 'tourists from the south arrive in the newly independent state' is countered by 'the bridge' and a consideration of both stories reveals both the impossibility of total separation and the ambiguities of union. The bridge itself is not a pleasant or even safe place to be; for Fiona and Charlie it indicates moving apart rather than coming together. It forces them both to consider where and how they look, and this clarifies the relationship between movement and perspective that Galloway explores in her other stories.

Can Scottish writing retain a sense of rootedness whilst at the same time reaching for a more fluid and adaptable vocabulary? Galloway's work suggests that there is now a literary space opening up in which writers can explore and draw on this dynamic between place and identity. Such writing moves beyond resistance towards a recognition of the space that is Scotland—a recognition that is at once creative, positive and open.

---

16. Compare this to Susan Sontag's observation: 'the camera makes everyone a tourist in other people's reality, and eventually in one's own'. *New York Review of Books*, 18 April 1974.

Melting Moments

The empathic self in *The Trick is to Keep Breathing*

Carolyn Masel

One of the most compelling aspects of Galloway's fiction is her insistence on the primacy of experience, an insistence that seems all the more remarkable given her predilection for formal experimentation. Such experiments usually imply a self-conscious literariness, yet it is life as it is lived at the most empirical level—responses to sensual stimuli and reflections on those responses—that shapes Galloway's narrators and the stories they tell. There is a fundamental honesty in this mode of writing that has nothing to do with confession; on the contrary, Galloway puts her writing on the line by requiring us to measure her narrators' life experience against our own. The response she encourages in her readers is thus more than usually empathic, where empathy is defined as an acquired understanding of another's experience, as distinct from sympathy, which involves an identification with another's emotional response. Whilst it has been argued that all reading is a fundamentally empathic activity, in *The Trick is to Keep Breathing* and some of her short stories, Galloway's capacity to elicit an empathic response in the reader amounts to a strategy, an essential part of her narrative method:

> Large hands were uncovering something from inside brown paper, carefully. There was someone moving around in here, thinking her unconscious. Lying prone in the half-dark Mhairi stiffened. The too-close

wall was making goosepimples along her arm, her nerves bristling. Like her skin was contracting, trying to make less of itself. Under the covers, the tee-shirt was rucked to her waist. She was half-asleep, belly-naked. Prone. The sound came again, tickling the hair on the back of her neck. The crackle of someone unwrapping a claw hammer. A length of cable.

Cheesewire.[1]

Reading Galloway means being constantly reminded that reading is a gendered activity. When the narrating subject or the centre of consciousness is feminine, which is most of the time in her work, comparing one's own experience to that of her feminine subjects is, inevitably, to invoke one's own gender politics. Her emphasis on sensory experience and perceptions arising from it may well be informed by feminist narratives of self-discovery of the 1970s, and the overall shape of her first novel, with its drawn-out psychological decline and sharp rise, might seem also to conform to a '70s pattern. But one of Galloway's most skilfully drawn narrating subjects, Joy, in *The Trick is to Keep Breathing*, seems much more than a representative case study, and eliciting empathy rather than sympathy, understanding rather than identification, is an altogether colder mode of operating.

The essence of eliciting an empathic response lies in indirection. Where, in the nineteenth century, a writer could demand empathy at a particular juncture by directly addressing the reader, a postmodern reader is just as likely to distance him/herself from the text on such occasions. Even when one's gender and circumstances approximate those of the intended addressee, when addressed as a Gentle Reader (*Jane Eyre*) or a mother (*Uncle Tom's Cabin*), one tends to evade the confrontation, assume some other reader is intended; indeed, the technique of direct address seems to be one of the things that date the novels that assume the right to it so decisively. By contrast, contemporary addresses to the reader tend to be self-conscious, fully aware of the oddity of address as a literary technique:

> A story is like a letter. *Dear You,* I'll say. Just *you,* without a name.
> Attaching a name attaches *you* to the world of fact, which is riskier, more hazardous: who knows what the chances are out there, of survival, yours?
> I will say *You, you,* like an old love song …

---

1. *Where You Find It*, p.45

I'll pretend you can hear me.

But it's no good, because I know you can't.[2]

In this passage from *The Handmaid's Tale*, Margaret Atwood engages the reader's attention precisely by troping on the impossibility of communication, dramatising her narrator at the bars of the prison that is text. Indeed, this passage stands out in the novel as a highly self-conscious moment, a self-reflexive moment that images the isolated freedom of the writer as much as her protagonist.

In Galloway, the prison of text is more like a dungeon. *The Trick is to Keep Breathing* opens with a passage that might at first seem to resemble a confession, suggesting a permeable barrier between narrator and reader. It soon becomes apparent, however, that the confusion that is being meticulously documented is not being so treated for the sake of explanation or any other quasi-communicatory purpose. Moreover, the 'you' here clearly means 'I';[3] Galloway's self is more enclosed, more sealed off even than Atwood's enslaved protagonist:

I can't remember the last week with any clarity.

I want to be able to remember it because it was the last time anything was in any way unremarkable. Eating and drinking routinely, sleeping when I wanted to. It would be nice to remember but I don't.

Now I remember everything all the time. You never know what you might need to recollect later, when the significance of the moment might appear. They never give you any warning.

They never give you any warning. (p. 6)

The little shock that registers with that last line is a shock of recognition: that acknowledging the absence of a warning must itself serve as that warning. Like any recognition, it involves two agencies, irrespective of whether they are merely two aspects of the self—here, the measuring self, the documentary 'I', taking heed of the knowing self, the 'you' who knows 'you never know'. And it is not just the narrator who is dramatised in the process of suddenly

---

2. Margaret Atwood, *The Handmaid's Tale* (Toronto: McClelland and Stewart, 1985), p. 50.

3. I would argue that, while it is grammatically possible for the 'you' to be a colloquial form of 'one', the personal situation depicted here is too specific to admit of generalization.

knowing something; the reader, too, experiences a kind of double-take. The repeated line cannot be read in the same way as the line before. The result is a swift opening out into alarm, into unbounded presentness: now is the anticipated significant moment and it is a moment without end. Yet, in the final analysis, Galloway does not breach the usual contract between reader and writer; the reader's status remains that of an over-hearer, not a direct addressee.

The kind of self-consciousness elicited in the reader through direct address, or any other breaching of the reader–writer contract, would be inimical to Galloway's method. On the contrary, what is required of us as readers is an unusual degree of what Keats famously called '*Negative Capability*': 'that is when man is capable of being in uncertainties, Mysteries, doubts, without any irritable reaching after fact & reason...',[4] a passive state of heightened receptivity that Keats illustrates with a parable of the bee and the flower:

> It has been an old Comparison for our urging on—the Bee hive—
> however it seems to me that we should rather be the flower than the
> Bee—for it is a false notion that more is gained by receiving than
> giving... let us not therefore go hurrying about and collecting honey-bee
> like, buzzing here and there impatiently from a knowledge of what is to
> be arrived at: but let us open our leaves like a flower and be passive and
> receptive—budding patiently under the eye of Apollo and taking hints
> from every noble insect that favours us with a visit...[5]

If the reader did not possess that heightened capacity for empathy, reading some of the short stories or *The Trick is to Keep Breathing* s/he would soon acquire it, for the reason that those narrators themselves are unusually empathic. It is their own capacity to empathise with other characters in a given narrative that enlists our empathy as readers; we need it in order to make sense of what we are overhearing. The creation of empathic narrators dramatically increases the capacity for empathy that we 'ordinarily' require as readers:

> Mona liked looking at Danny and you only got to look at somebody
> properly when they were distracted, not knowing you were watching. You

---

4.   Letter to George and Thomas Keats, 21, 27? December 1817; in Keats, 261.
5.   Letter to John Hamilton Reynolds, 19 February 1818; in Keats, 265-6.

got to read things they didn't necessarily know they were telling you. Right now, he looked that way he did when a concert was over and he thought he'd done ok.[6]

The work of J. Brooks Bouson, whose analyses of various novels are informed by her practice as a clinical psychologist, adds another dimension to my rather commonsensical account. Her approach is derived from the work of the psychoanalyst Heinz Kohut, whose interest in narcissism and in the neediness manifested by narcissistic patients drew him away from his early Freudianism. His theory, as summarised by Bouson, begins with the articulation of a bipolar self, whose two poles manifest what were originally infantile desires:

> The *archaic grandiose self* is rooted in the infant's feelings that he or she is the center of the world and all-powerful and that the parents are there to meet every need and demand. *Archaic idealization* finds its source in the infant's experience of being nurtured, held, and soothed by the parents.
>
> In normal development, the child's archaic grandiosity and exhibitionism, empathically responded to by the *mirroring* (i.e., echoing, approving, confirming) parents, is gradually tamed as it is undercut by reality… Similarly, idealizing needs are slowly undercut by reality as the child… experiences gradual and phase-appropriate disappointments in the idealized parent imago(s).[7]

On the other hand, the child whose needs have not been satisfied may evolve certain compensatory strategies, and these may persist into adulthood. In many cases these strategies are ineffectual in the restoration of self-esteem and self-motivation; however, in the context of psychoanalysis the patient may be given the opportunity to replay his or her unfulfilled needs. In the course of analysis, a patient may well come to view an analyst as a parent-figure that s/he seeks to merge with or perform for ('transference'), and the analyst may respond with his/her own inevitable projections ('countertransference'). It is this process of countertransference—the set of emotional responses of the analyst to the patient—that is, broadly speaking,

---

6. *Where You Find It*, p. 23
7. J. Brooks Bouson, *The Empathic Reader: A Study of the Narcissistic Character and the Drama of the Self* (Amherst: The University of Mass. Press, 1989), p. 14.

analogous to the relationship between reader and text in a given instance.[8]

Bouson's analogy points up both the centrality and the limitations of an empathic response. Empathy may be essential, but empathy alone is not enough; a capacity for self-reflection is equally necessary. Without it, the analyst stands to harm the patient through responding inappropriately. Apparently, one of the characteristic behaviours of apprentice analysts is the re-enactment of various aspects of a given patient's feelings and/or behaviour. A reader, too, may demonstrate an inadequate understanding of a given text by tending to replicate, rather than analyse, precisely those aspects of the text that have not been understood—something we can see in the work of apprentice critics. According to Bouson, both of these behaviours can be understood as forms of repetition compulsion.[9]

Extending this analogy to cover an empathic narrator such as Joy in *The Trick is to Keep Breathing* could conceivably produce the following scenario. The reader's capacity for empathy (equivalent to countertransference) is enlisted in response to a needy narrator (analysand) who, rather than engaging with us directly, responds as an empathic reader herself to the perceived neediness of other characters in her own attempt at countertransference. (It is crucial that the distinction between the dynamic relationship of actual analyst and analysand and the metaphorical relationship between narrator and reader be borne in mind here; I do not want to suggest that the process of writing a novel is analogous to therapy— such a reading would not only be pointlessly reductive, but also unethical and, in any case, unknowable.) Since Galloway's style of first person narration provides no access to the interiority of other characters, they will remain ciphers, beyond our capacity for empathy. Hence, we are both reliant upon the narrator's skill as a reader and required to assess it. The analogy is thus probably closer to the debriefing of a practice analyst by another, senior practitioner in the absence of patients. What a model derived from Bouson's psychological model usefully provides is an opportunity for the reader to intervene in the course of empathically apprehending the other's experience, where intervention involves evaluation, and includes, I have suggested, bringing one's gender politics to bear on the account as it unfolds.

I want to explore these ideas about the empathic narrator in *The Trick is to Keep Breathing* initially by discussing quite a sizable section of the beginning

---

8.   Ibid., p. 24.
9.   Ibid., p. 25.

of the book, whose disjunct passages together constitute a sort of 'first movement'. In the course of this discussion, I shall seek to demonstrate that what starts off as an apparent capacity to feel with or on behalf of another proves to be a valuable technique for constructing a comprehensive indictment of the largest social forces. A narrator who is given to measuring makes a good diagnostician.

First, however, it needs to be said that constant reference to 'the narrator' or 'the narrating subject' may be misleading in that it implies a wholeness of the self that is certainly not present in Galloway's first novel. Over the course of more than a hundred years we have become so accustomed to feminine selves as fractured constructions that the very notion of the fractured subject has become a cliché. Indeed, we might argue that a feminine self that did not register the immense pressures of attempting to exist in language, as in the world, might be judged insufficiently reflective, even when that response involves what seems a self-damaging dispersal. Thus, narrative fragmentation can be seen as a sign of authenticity and evidence of it is often valued, whether as a revolutionary disruption of the symbolic order or the telling incoherence of *écriture féminine*. The best place to study the strategic working of the fragmentary subject is probably the three novels, for there subjectivity is extended and sustained. There are a number of ways one might do this. One would be to foreground the pattern of incoherence, illuminating the sharp edges of the fractured subject against a notional wholeness. Another way would be to look at what kind of narrative can be constituted from the juxtaposed fragments themselves: to be content with parts and an absent unity. This latter option suits my purpose here, since I want to show how those fragments accumulate to build a narrating subject who consistently negotiates with largely inimical forces.

In addition to the material fragments of which *The Trick is to Keep Breathing* is composed, there is, as we have seen already in the italicised opening passage with its self-reflexive warning, a fracture in the self as ego, evinced by the two pronouns ('I' and 'you') reflecting two aspects of subjectivity. In the passage that immediately follows it, the self is perceived to be disjunct, with the disjunction registering as a doubling: 'I watch myself from the corner of the room / sitting in the armchair, at the foot of the stairwell'. The dislocated pieces are perceived as incongruent, like '[t]he curtains [that] are too wee to close properly...'. One hardly recognises the diction of the body in the *arm* of armchair and *foot* of stairwell until further disparate body parts register: the wet shoe, the foot rocking back and forth in the wet until it skids and jerks her knee, knuckles that rust from clutching the armrests. Getting up is a mechanical event:

> I have to concentrate: one finger at a time, releasing pressure and rebalancing in the chair to accommodate the tilting, adjusting, redistributing pieces of myself. Hands are bastards: so many separate pieces. The muscles in the thighs tightening as the feet push down and the stomach clenching to take the weight then I'm out the chair, shaky but upright. My knees ache. I move, ignoring the carpet as it tries to nudge through the soles. (p. 8)

In this state, one may well strive for the unfeelingness of things or even of art: 'slic[ing] between the quilt and the mattress, making myself flat like cardboard'. We should note that, perturbingly, caring for oneself means disposing of oneself (disposing of one's own troublesome superfluous contours, or posing as a disposable cardboard character). And all because Joy 'read in a magazine once' about the best way to get warm (p. 8), as though well-being could be attained by following instructions. We should note Joy's readiness to cede authority to the written word, for that particular method of undermining her autonomy will prove a significant factor later in the novel.

In an environment where nothing seems natural (getting up from a chair, lying in bed) or congruent (the too-short curtains, getting up at 03:25 in order to go to bed), other patterns insidiously establish themselves: for example, things acquire accretions which need to be stripped away ('[T]he black sleeve of my jacket…is furry with white from the [bed]covers', '[l]eaves are cramping the drain' (p. 10)). Predictably enough in this world of dislocated parts, the mirror in the bathroom reveals a grotesquerie, 'a kneeling torso, head chopped off sheer at the white plastic rim', viewed from the perspective of a peeping tom ('like looking through a window at someone else'). Despite all this, a tiny residue of *amour propre* leads her to conceive of the washing away of sweat as making her sweet, (p. 10) a minimal sign that she wishes herself well.

The imagery of dislocation is picked up again in the description of the narrator's house. First, there is a gap between expectation and actuality: 'When I was small I always wanted a red front door. This front door is bottle green.' (p. 14) Then there is a split in the narrator's self-perception: 'I have to rummage through my bag and every pocket while I stand at the door as though I'm begging to be mugged.' The double vantage here is of victim and mugger. Typically, the self-judgement is a harsh one: Joy's vulnerability is a fault ('begging to be mugged'). If, as sometimes happens, only one aspect of this persistent double perspective is apparent, that does not mean unity has been achieved; signs may disappear, but their scars remain, like the two pairs of dots left by the house numbers, or a childish wish for a red front door, or—in the earlier bath scene—the pink scar, which only appears 'like invisible ink' in warm water. We are inscribed by our experience and memory is the scar. Or, as Joy puts it later, 'Myra left marks. None of them show'. (p. 59)

Reminder notes to oneself also indicate disjunction. Although their intention is benign, they may be worse than useless: 'Could be an old one: it's hard to tell.' (p. 11) Hard to tell, too, if the clock has stopped. The theme of time's imperviousness to all attempts to measure it is extended from the private to the public sphere—from Joy's home to the school where she teaches—with the result that what starts off as a diagnosis of a personal sense of being unwell becomes a diagnosis of a wider malaise. The sign on the school door—a public version of her reminder notes—announces VISITORS MUST REPORT TO THE OFFICE, but it turns out that 'The office is open and nobody looks up', suggesting a bureaucracy that is compelling in theory but negligent in practice. In the school environment, art has almost completely replaced nature ('All the lights are on downstairs because the corridors are dark all day'), yet traces of the organic persist: the passing of time registers as a change of smell from hospital to gymnasium. The painting in the stairwell combines both elements. It depicts 'some kind of fantasy domestic scene… with mummy in the kitchen and dad in the garage [while] offspring lie in bed or watch tv or play on a snake-green lawn'. (p. 11) It's that snake-green lawn, lurid yet Edenic, that gives the game away: there is surely no better image for the unlikelihood of such a paradise.

The social indictment widens into the masterly description of the Bourtree Hill estate (known to its residents as Boot Hill):

> Boot Hill is a new estate well outside the town it claims to be part of. There was a rumour when they started building the place that it was meant for undesirables: difficult tenants from other places, shunters, overspill from Glasgow. That's why it's so far away from everything. (p. 13)

This is dislocation on a grand scale. And the collective social intention that underlies it seems far from benign. The plan of the estate is so bad, so much worse than ineffectual, that the most charitable thing that can be said about the planners is that they were too mentally separate from the results of their work for it to have any hope of success:

> Boot Hill is full of tiny, twisty roads, wild currant bushes to represent the great outdoors, pubs with plastic beer glasses and kids. The twisty roads are there to prevent the kids being run over. The roads are meant to make drivers slow down so they get the chance to see and stop in time. This is a dual misfunction. Hardly anyone has a car. If one does appear on the horizon, the kids use the bends to play chicken, deliberately lying low and leaping out at the last minute for fun. The roads end up more conducive to child death than if they had been straight. What they do achieve is to make the buses go slow. Buses are infrequent so the shelters are covered in graffiti and kids hanging from the roofs. Nobody waits in these shelters even when it's raining. It rains a lot. The buses take a long time. (p. 13)

The safety features on this estate misfire because of the compound failure of imagination on the part of the planners. First, '[h]ardly anyone has a car': people are poorer than the authorities managed to envisage. Secondly, people—at least, children—are infinitely more resourceful than the patronising provision made for them. The bus shelters conceived as civic structures are merely sad monuments to the authorities' failure to plan effectively. Yet, 'covered with graffiti and kids hanging from the roofs', they are transformed by the dwellers of Boot Hill into quasi-tropical emblems of a continuing imaginative life. What the reader comes to suspect about good intentions that fail because of the failure of imagination is that they were never good enough in the first place. There is some kind of moral failing involved, whether insouciance or bad faith. Part of the reason we come to suspect this is because Joy's attitude toward others is far from consistent; her goodwill is also subject to intermittent failure.

This first becomes apparent in an early, explicit statement about the experience of self-division and doubling: 'The good thing is that I need not be present when I am working. I can be outside myself, watching from the corner of the room.' (p. 12) This kind of experience of doubleness is often associated with an outstanding performance, and if teaching drama—which is what Joy does—only involved performing, we could take this at face value as the mark of a good teacher. But the notion of an absent-spirited teacher is altogether more perturbing. Knowing what we do about the watcher in the corner—the watcher of the self as it wakes in the armchair at the foot of the stairs—it seems unlikely that the watcher in the corner of the classroom will be that transcendent aspect of self that conducts or directs the performing self; it seems rather more likely to be a passive aspect of self that is merely waiting for the teaching self to finish—a patient aspect of self, that endures.

The doubleness that involves some sort of duplicity is also evident in Joy's dealings with her friend's mother, Ellen, and in her dealings with the Health Visitor. In the former case, duplicity is inextricable from the bereavement-induced eating disorder that is part of Joy's general neediness—that is, precisely that aspect of her character that makes the comparison with an analysand such an apt one. There is no malevolence in her relationship with this borrowed mother, but her illness nevertheless inevitably leads to deception:

HEALTH UPDATE: ULTIMATE DIET

By this time, not eating has become so rewarding you won't want to stop. And who can blame you? But avoiding food is harder than you'd think. Repeated refusing starts to look rude and thoughtless. You know it's important they shouldn't see the deliberateness of your choice and indeed, sometimes it's hard not to develop a degree of paranoia in view of how persistent some people can be! (p. 85)

The session with the Health Visitor—a key episode in the novel's first movement—involves another kind of duplicity altogether. This is a case not of compulsive but of deliberate deception, deception as a chosen mode of defence. Moreover, it is a mode of defence that we understand to be absolutely necessary, such is Galloway's skill in recruiting our empathy. In fact, our empathic response is twofold: first, the narrator recruits the reader's empathy on her own behalf; then, she enlists us as allies against the obtuse Health Visitor. Although Joy has almost two hours to prepare for the Health Visitor's arrival—preparation which she describes as 'a set routine so I don't need to think' (p. 17)—the time seems to slip away unnoticed (during the recounting of what does need thinking about), so that 'By twenty past [ten minutes before her appointment] I'm running along the twisty road between the houses to shop for biscuits' (p. 19). We feel she should not have to run this obstacle course, given her care to measure the time and the exertion of control represented by her cleaning the kitchen and the living room, and that this loss of time, despite every precaution, signals an alarming lack of control over her environment. Given the stubborn unamenability of that environment, we can understand why she should attempt to outmanoeuvre it. By implicating the Health Visitor in the environment, Galloway makes us complicit in Joy's attempts to outmanoeuvre her. She buys 'different [biscuits] each time hoping they are something else she will enjoy', but enjoyment in this context can only mean, at best, a form of compensation for the dishonesty that characterises their relationship; less nobly, Joy wants to distract her from her ostensible task of listening.[10] Whilst the Health Visitor is described at one point as 'waddl[ing]' (p. 23), an indication that she is liable to be fobbed off in precisely this way, it is in this very area also that Joy seeks to manifest tight control over her life ('I can't be trusted with custard creams so deliberately don't get them' (p. 19)). Here, in recounting her first session with the Health Visitor, in which she made a genuine attempt to communicate her distress, Joy demonstrates both the fragility of her own self-control and a sense of its being oddly connected with the Health Visitor's unreliable self-control:

> She was dunking a gingernut. I watched her hand rocking back and forth, getting the saturation just right. At the crucial moment, she flipped the biscuit to her mouth, sucking off the soaked part, her tongue worming out for a dribble of tea. It missed. The dribble ran down to her chin and she coughed, giggling. I knew if I opened my mouth something terrible would dribble out like the tea, gush down the front of my shirt, over her shoes and cover the carpet like
> like
> like (p. 22)

The first part of this passage seems like a prime example of empathy in the narrator. Her intrigue with the technique of biscuit dunking, however, is not strictly empathic, but is born of her own suppressed hunger. She has trouble taking things in and, like the Health Visitor, in keeping them in. Moreover, it is impossible not to acknowledge that, seen in this Brobdignagian detail, the Health Visitor is repulsive ('her tongue *worming out...*'). Her physical crassness is seen to be an extension of her mentality. There can be no doubt that she deserves to be duped, for she herself is duplicitous in a small kind of

---

10. Perceptive readers will note that 'melting moments', the biscuits featured in my title, do not appear in Galloway's text. Joy buys well-known packaged biscuits, whereas melting moments tend to be homemade. Nevertheless, since 'melting moments' seemed appropriate to the general topic of empathy, I hope I may be forgiven this small licence.

way, invariably exclaiming with surprise when Joy invariably brings out tea and biscuits (p. 21), or pretending genuine interest in Joy's well-being. But while the Health Visitor is much too dim to win what Joy resentfully calls 'this fucking game', the game still has to be played, for the alternative, which Joy tried once, is unthinkable. We can quite understand why Joy would not repeat the mistake of attempting to make a confidante of someone tactless enough to announce: '"You can tell me anything you like. I assure you it goes no further and I've heard it all before."' (p. 23)

Despite all this, as soon as the Health Visitor stands up to leave, Joy finds that 'guilt is spoiling the relief'. It is up to the reader to deduce what she might be feeling guilty about. One possibility is that she feels guilty about her own dishonesty, which, if we deem it to be justified by the Health Visitor's dishonesty, means that her guilt can be read as an indication of an overly nice conscience and can be laid to her credit. Alternatively, she could conceivably feel guilt toward the doctor who sent the Health Visitor 'out of love' (p. 20). In support of this, as the Health Visitor walks out the door, the narrator seems to hear a message, 'You Always Expect Too Much', but it is impossible to tell whether the 'you' refers to herself or to the Health Visitor. If 'you' in effect means 'I', the guilt would be about not having made the most of the opportunity to communicate, despite the Health Visitor's manifest failings as a listener—as if, despite all the inauspicious signs, Joy could not help hoping the official visit would make a difference. But if 'you' means the Health Visitor, then Joy is more straightforwardly acknowledging a sense of her own inadequacy. Indeed, what the reader tends to register, above all, is the indeterminacy of the addressee, with its implicit suggestion of a narratorly impulse to merge with the Health Visitor. The responsibility for the failure of their meeting cannot, in the end, be ascribed to either one of them; it is shared, and it is this shared sense that gives Galloway's description of the final departure of the Health Visitor a luminous, poetic quality: 'The exhaust rattles till she curves out of sight, struggling against her bulk and the need to turn the wheel.' (pp. 23–4) The exhaust is as much psychic as mechanical; the Health Visitor's body is as distorted as the narrator's; she, too, needs to take control of her destiny.

What I have described as the novel's first movement culminates in the narrator's visit to the local Tesco. In a parallel construction to the description of her house, what is first described here is the exterior—the huge red neon sign—and then the exterior of the items: the packaging: 'rows of pretty boxes' and 'silver polythene skins begging to be burst'. The items in that house of plenty, that cornucopia, are catalogued in a way that recalls Nicole's shopping frenzy in F. Scott Fitzgerald's *Tender is the Night*. The randomness of Nicole's purchases in that book[11] is echoed here in the incongruity of the foods that are found together—in this case merely because of the way they are processed. Hence, '[t]he adrenalin smell of coffee drifts and draws towards… the wedges of Edam, Stilton and Danish Blue'; fingers are numbed equally on 'bags of frozen broccoli and solid chocolate gateaux'. Blueberry pie filling is found, at least on the page, next to papaya and mango (p. 25).

The challenge of making a set piece about shopping effective is the challenge of originality. When the shop is a supermarket, the meaning inevitably has something to do with the display and consumption of dreams and the terrible depersonalisation that the consumer culture effects. Galloway's short piece works because of its small fresh touches. First of all, she makes the point that consumption does not necessarily mean buying. Indeed, 'I don't encourage buying', Joy says, treating herself like a child to be diplomatically managed. And there are games about choosing that one can play, such as 'teasing [one]self with the labels', even if the decision is a foregone conclusion. After the deprived environments she has previously described—the Boot Hill estate and her house in particular—the plenitude of the supermarket is something to be enjoyed; once again, the challenge for the narrator is to outmanoeuvre authoritarian tactics and categories.

Considered in this light, the movement over the course of this short passage is from success to failure. After the games and the feeling of wealth and leisure comes a more equivocal passage about buying a new magazine. Joy represents herself as 'get[ting] excited when I see a new cover smiling over the chewing gum and chocolate at the checkout racks', so it is up to the reader to register the capitulation apparently involved in this response. Equipped with magazine, Joy negotiates the precinct, her heels echoing confidently, but she also feels vulnerable to skateboard riders and rush hour pedestrians '[l]ike clockwork toys'. She herself appears to have successfully resisted automatism, but that is a fleeting triumph, for waiting for a break in the stream of

---

11. F. Scott Fitzgerald, *Tender is the Night*, pp. 54–5:
   'Nicole bought from a great list that ran two pages, and bought the things in the windows besides. Everything she liked that she couldn't possibly use herself, she bought as a present for a friend. She bought colored beads, folding beach cushions, artificial flowers, honey, a guest bed, bags, scarfs, love birds, miniatures for a doll's house and three yards of some new cloth the color of prawns. She bought a dozen bathing suits, a rubber alligator, a travelling chess set of leather jackets of kingfisher blue and burning bush from Hermes . . .'

clockwork toys makes her feel '[a]s though I'm trapped in a coop full of hens for the slaughterhouse.' The choice of roles here is disheartening: heedless mechanism or doomed creature.

But things get worse. From here, we proceed to the nub of the matter: 'Today, the important thing is not to think about the Health Visitor and just keep moving. I lied. No-one is visiting tonight.' The admission of this face-saving or distracting lie is initially perhaps less interesting to the reader than the admission of the lack of contact. For it is at this point that it becomes clear that lack of contact is the theme that unifies the whole of the TESCO passage. The episode ends with a parody of the need for contact; the sense of touch is pre-empted and diverted at every point:

> At the end of the precinct, a security guard opens the doors with a leather glove and offers me a sweetie. I smile and take it. Round the corner I drop it in a plastic bin shaped like a rabbit.
>
> Bobby the Bunny says Keep your Country Tidy. (p. 25)

All of the details here resonate. What kind of security can be provided by a security guard—especially when he needs to protect himself from direct contact with the doors that it is his task to open? The plastic bin is shaped like an animal that is soft to the touch. The game the narrator plays is, by this point, familiar to the reader: it is to pretend to accept what is offered, while actually having none of it. Detail by detail, her acknowledgement that '[she] tell[s] lies all the time' acquires a deeper meaning. It is no longer a matter of deceiving the Health Visitor, or even of not having visitors of any kind. It is a matter of dwelling in a whole culture that lies—that wears leather gloves and offers sweeties, that numbs the fingers equally with frozen broccoli and frozen gateaux. Bobby the Bunny tropes on a notion of the pastoral, but there is no vestige of it here. His address to the masses is to Keep your Country Tidy, but no country is specified (unless Bobby the Bunny is code for Scotland the Victim), for he himself is an emblem of anonymous mass-production that goes beyond national boundaries, proliferating endlessly across the globe.

I have traced the 'first movement' of the novel in order to show how empathy functions as a strategy; but—in relation to the Health Visitor and the security guard at TESCO, for example—we have also seen it represented as a theme. This thematic aspect is developed further in relation to those official practitioners of empathy, the Health Professionals. Galloway's treatment of them is almost always ironic. The manifest incompetence of the Health Visitor is exceeded only by the Kafka-esque performance of Doctors One, Two and Three in the psychiatric hospital. But whilst their interchanges with the narrator may be farcical, it is a farce that does not efface the pain their incompetence causes:

DR THREE What sort of treatment do you want?
PATIENT I don't know. What do you suggest?
DR THREE Ah but that's the whole point. I'm not suggesting anything. You asked to see me and now you're wasting my time.
PATIENT [Hit where it hurts] OK. What about counselling? Or analysis? ECT even. How should I know?
DR THREE Don't be ridiculous.
PATIENT What am I supposed to do, then. Give me some sort of clue.
DR THREE What does everyone else do?
PATIENT They stop asking. (p. 164)

It is in dialogues such as this one that the utter ludicrousness of the merely reactive, professionally passive stance becomes clear—though the final note here is perhaps more Beckett than Kafka. Yet underlying the predominantly comic bleakness, a point is being made about falsity; the detachment of the professional empathiser can be learned:

PATIENT [Inspiration] Dr Three? Are you OK?
DR THREE What? What? [Looks as though he's just lost something]
PATIENT Are you OK? How's your head?
DR THREE How's what? [He looks childlike with confusion.]
PATIENT Your head. I heard you get these headaches.
DR THREE Pah. [Face back to normal] My wellbeing is not your concern. Leave. (p. 165)

This hollowness at the heart of things is everywhere in the novel. It is the source of all Joy's suffering, the condition from which, it would appear, no one can release her. But there is one even more serious lesson that she is destined to learn, and that lesson has to do with actively assuming meaninglessness, or acquiescing in the leeching away of meaning. The depiction of rape is probably always shocking, but what contributes to the particular shock of Joy's rape by Tony is the part that empathy plays in that event. For it is no distortion to say that Joy's being raped is represented as a consequence of her empathy, albeit an extreme consequence:

> He fished out a poke of crisps from under the counter and unzipped them, leaning back to think. Maybe we could have a meal. Go dancing.
>   Tony, I said. Why do you never take your wife?
> He looked offended.
>   She has her own friends, he said. She does all right.
>
> I felt bad afterwards. No matter what I do, I usually feel bad afterwards. Look, I thought, Tony is not a bad man. He's being kind. I should accept kindness for what it is, do more to help myself. And David has exams soon: he could do with the time to study. I must not cling. I must accept invitations etc etc. The callbox at the end of the road hove into view. Tony said he would collect me at seven.

sometime
presentim
that stop
before it t
late but o
ignore the

(pp. 173–4)

> He couldn't find a way inside my dress. I undid the buttons myself to make it quicker.

worst happ
we can onl
blame

Is this what you want? I said. Will this keep you happy? (p. 175)

> I have to go to work. Tony will be there. A dozen or so half-formed excuses and diversionary tactics could be gone into but they merely mask the essential fact. I have to go. I have to look him in the eye. Look, people make mistakes. They happen to everyone. You should be able to allow for mistakes and know that's all they are. Just because last week
>   because he
>   just because (p. 205)

It is this event that brings home to her the limits of that capacity to understand another person whilst remaining non-judgmental. Tony, who enters the novel early on, is never represented as anything other than a coarse and predatory figure, but since Joy is astute and streetwise, he does not seem unduly threatening. It is only when she chooses to abandon her customary defences, preferring, for some reason, to follow instructions in a book, that she ends up second-guessing the intuitions that have enabled her to survive thus far (pp. 173–4).

The key question here is why she should fall back, in this crucial moment, on the authority of the written word ('I must not cling. I must accept invitations etc etc'). The most cynical reading would entail her secret or unconscious desire for Tony, which the book provides her with an excuse to act out. I mention this only to set it aside as preposterous—since almost every utterance suggests Tony's brutality and Joy's belief that a person with the most minimal powers of perception would behave more honourably. Galloway leaves clues to a different interpretation. For one thing, reverting to written instructions would seem to be a habit of Joy's. We have already seen how, at the beginning of the novel, the way she lay in bed was determined by something she once read in a magazine about the best way to get warm. The question then arises as to whether Joy is naïve enough to believe something because she reads it in a book. From what we know of her, this would seem unlikely. Her verdict on herself bespeaks honesty, self-analysis, self-awareness:

> The defendant is anxious, depressed, mildly paranoiac and suffering from low self-image. Also guilty about all of these things and why not? The defendant refuses to see the Point or to accept what must be accepted whilst being fully apprised of the facts. (p. 200)

Furthermore, Joy's summary of the book in question, which is a book about bereavement, is extremely satirical. The book as she summarises it feels authentic, as though penned by someone so enmired in the methodology of counselling as to be deaf to self-irony. In addition, the context that the author assumes is so far off the mark—just like the assumptions of the planners of the Boot Hill estate—that further irony results. For example, chapter three's promise that 'my family will be a source of great strength and comfort if I let them' (p. 171) is either meaningless or painful, since both of Joy's parents are dead, and the banal reminder, 'Blood is thicker than water', is somewhat ominous, given her sister Myra's penchant for violence.

But the really telling detail is Joy's brief remark:

> I read the book in two and a half hours and cry all the way
> through.
> Like watching Bambi. (p. 172)

Saccharine, sentimental, clearly a fantasy world, but providing the opportunity for a good cry nonetheless—it is evident that reading the book is a kind of game. My point lies not so much in the voluntarism that playing a game entails as in the nature of the game itself. For a skilful player, or viewer, or a strong reader, will be one who is capable of deriving the optimum meaning from a text—that is, in Coleridgean terms, someone who can willingly suspend disbelief, or, in Keatsian terms, someone negatively capable, or, in terms of the current discussion, an empathic reader. We might think at first that the emotional detachment that distinguishes empathy from sympathy is missing, yet perhaps that is not entirely the case: the recognition that the world of the bereavement book is as innocent as Bambi's—that it cannot be confused with the actual world—is possibly what occasions Joy's tears. This interpretation is consistent with a view of Joy as an accurate reader of the world, a probing diagnostician, a realist. And it also consistent with Joy's own admission that, from time to time, she knowingly partakes of the world's fictions. Yet this world, this consensus of lies, is not a world from which anyone can be exempted: the choices are only to be a clever or a clumsy participant. Tony, as unperceptive and insensitive as it is possible to be, nevertheless appears to respond to the song on his Country and Western tape that he lacks the wit to interpret:

> *When you think I've loved you all I can*
> *I'm gonna love you a little bit more* (p. 174)

The essential difference between Tony and Joy, then, lies in their capacity for empathy, where empathy entails, among other things, the acknowledgment of boundaries. You cannot empathise with someone whose otherness you do not admit, and Tony is so self-serving that he can neither observe a personal boundary, nor even perceive a need for one. Yet despite the moral repugnance one feels for him, he is not, I think, a sinister figure so much as a figure of limitation, a fragment of the world-at-large, commercialised and commodifying. As for Joy, if, *in extremis*, her only option appears to be to cooperate in order to get the rape over quickly, that solution, she learns, is not a repeatable one. Sooner or later, she has to make Tony understand what NO means (p. 209). The lesson they learn about the necessity for boundaries—boundaries that can be trusted and that will be respected—is, then, is essentially the same one.

Galloway's world in *The Trick is to Keep Breathing* is bleak, but it is not unremittingly so. Against the darkness of an insufficiently humane set of worldly authorities is set the genuine goodwill of a number of characters. Dr Stead seems neither more competent nor less hard-pressed than any of the other doctors in the novel, yet Joy respects him, feels responsible for disappointing him when the drugs he prescribes prove ineffective. This is a further instance of Joy's capacity for empathy—but one gets the sense that Dr Stead's concern for her wellbeing is genuine, and that he takes the manifest failure of his course of treatment to heart. Even less ambivalent are the two truly nurturing spirits of the novel, Marianne Holmes and her mother Ellen. Marianne's benignity is manifested as a series of cheering texts—postcards from the States, lists of things to do to pass the time until Joy feels better (pp. 16, 37). Ellen's domesticity, and particularly her 'need to feed', is treated with much humour, but, as I suggested earlier, entirely without malice (pp. 33, 85).

The easy allegiance of one woman to another in a world where relationships with men are difficult and unfulfilling is the subject of Galloway's second novel, *Foreign Parts*. However, the method of this novel is completely different. Empathy is hardly present at all, despite Cassie's and Rona's long familiarity with each other. Instead, what we tend to get is a good deal of writing about surfaces, bespeaking a relationship in which the boundaries between self and other—or, more accurately, between other and self—are well established and do not yield to any amount of curious scrutiny (pp. 60–1).[12] A door has closed; a self that was porous has been filled in, acquiring substance, solidity. *Foreign Parts* may be a much more mature and accomplished novel—yet it lacks precisely those visionary or resonant moments that are formed in the hollowness of the self.

---

12. The same thing is true of Galloway's most recent novel, *Clara*, for all that one might expect a woman dominated by her father and totally devoted to the well-being of her husband to demonstrate but a flimsy conception of boundaries. This is anything but the case.

Works cited

Atwood, Margaret (1985) *The Handmaid's Tale*. Toronto: McClelland and Stewart.

Bouson, J. Brooks (1989) *The Empathic Reader: A Study of the Narcissistic Character and the Drama of the Self*. Amherst: The University of Massachusetts Press.

Fitzgerald, F. Scott (1962) *Tender is the Night*. New York: Scribners.

Galloway, Janice (1991) *The Trick is to Keep Breathing*. London: Minerva [1989].

—— (1995) *Foreign Parts*. London: Random House.

—— (1996) *Where You Find It*. London: Jonathan Cape.

—— (2002) *Clara*. London: Jonathan Cape.

Keats, John (1959) *Selected Poems and Letters*. Douglas Bush (Ed.). Boston: Houghton Mifflin.

Onto plums
Spending 'A Week with Uncle Felix'

Willy Maley

The title tale of *Blood*, Janice Galloway's acclaimed short story collection, is rightly regarded as a contemporary classic, and has received considerable attention in essays and reviews. Less visited is the collection's last long story, 'A Week with Uncle Felix', an awkward and disturbing account of a young girl's visit to her uncle's house. In an authoritative critical overview of Galloway's work in *A History of Scottish Women's Writing* (Edinburgh University Press, 1997), Douglas Gifford touches on the story in question in ways that suggest it may be being under-read or even—heaven forefend!—misread. Since *A History of Scottish Women's Writing* is already regarded as a seminal work of criticism, it is important to tug at the sleeve, as it were, and remind readers that Galloway's fiction throws up the type of thorny problems that make summary readings a risky business. I spent a week with this story, mulling over its rich imagery. Like many extended endpieces in short story collections, it has the outline of an abandoned novel lurking in its tight folds, and may amount to a novella.

In his introduction to Galloway, Gifford describes *The Trick is to Keep Breathing* as 'one of the strongest new statements of the need to redefine the place of women in society' (Gifford 1997, p.607). My own feeling is that the message of Galloway's work is less that the place of women in society needs redefined, than that the place of men needs to be questioned. Galloway's project is to incite women to surge into forbidden quarters. When Gifford speaks of *The Trick is to Keep Breathing*, there is arguably a note of reproach in his commentary that is absent from Galloway's writing. For example, we are told that 'Joy, in failing to extend understanding to herself or to Michael's wife and family, is drowning in the subconscious guilt which she cannot articulate in order to come to terms with it' (Gifford 1997, p. 608). The same somewhat judgmental attitude is evident in the following remarks:

> Forced to follow Joy's interpretation of events, and perhaps becoming intolerant of her monotony of self-interest, the reader begins to realise that Joy is hiding something which lies behind all her tortured diary entries, her anorexia, her binges followed by vomiting, her use of sleazy men as escape, her solitary drinking and her introversion. This is that guilt, partly her own and partly induced and promoted by her society, concerning Paul, the man she lived with and left for Michael, and Michael's wife and family, and all her own buried familial guilt. Galloway doesn't allocate blame. Instead she simply shows Joy's subtle and unsubtle ostracisation, together with the guilt she feels, which must be externalised. (Gifford 1997, p. 608)

Leaving aside the matter of whether Joy left Paul for Michael, this is a judgmental summary. Joy's trouble is that she is internalising guilt. Society, specifically capitalist patriarchy, is really to blame.

Gifford goes on to refer to Galloway's typographical experimentation 'with thoughts printed in the margin to suggest the marginalisation of our deepest selves amidst the pressures of contemporary society' (Gifford 1997, p. 608). And there it is. We have travelled only a short distance from redefining the place of women in society to the marginalisation of 'our deepest selves' in contemporary society. Appropriation follows identification.

Gifford sees 'Need for Restraint', another of the stories from *Blood*, as being about 'a girl witnessing street violence being told so repeatedly by her man that it's nothing to do with her that she finally breaks down and they separate' (Gifford 1997, p. 609). In fact, the street violence the girl is witnessing is mirrored by the violence of her boyfriend, as he strikes a shop window: 'There was the dull thump of his fist against glass' (Galloway, 'Need for Restraint', p. 87). She later reflects that 'It had been a dark evening through long windows'. To be blind to this act of violence, this 'domestic' darkness, is to be blind to the need for restraint, and to miss the point of the story, and its connections to other stories, like 'Frostbite', in which a woman waiting at a bus stop is harangued by a drunk man, or 'Fearless', in which a maladjusted male attempts to intimidate a young girl out shopping with her mother.

The mother in 'Fearless', like the boyfriend in 'Need for Restraint', is complicit with this malevolence since she chooses to turn her back and make her daughter stare into a shop window rather than confront Fearless, who stands glowering behind them. The irony is that the girl can still clearly make out the seething figure reflected in the glass:

> We were standing facing a shop window, her hand in mine, thick through two layers of winter gloves. The shop window was full of fireplaces.
> (Galloway, 'Fearless', p.113)

The shop window in 'Fearless', like the shop window thumped by the boyfriend in 'Need for Restraint', functions as a mirror and a hammer, reflecting but also repeating the violence it is supposed to hold at arm's length. Fireplaces are unlikely to hold the attention of a young girl, especially if unlit, and the girl suspects that her mother shares her disinterest:

> It's unlikely she was actually interested in fireplaces: she was just doing what she was supposed to do in the hope he'd leave us alone—and teaching me to do the same. Fearless got closer. Then I saw his reflection in the glass: three days' growth, the bunnet, the taped-up specs.
> (Galloway, 'Fearless', p.114)

The girl turns round when Fearless directs foul and abusive language at her mother, sees him 'staring back with these pebble-glass eyes', and lashes out with her foot, striking him hard on the shin, and routing the bully. Despite her mother's warnings that she'll be 'found dead strangled up a close one day', the girl is alive and kicking at the story's close.

Glass and windows play a large part in Galloway's writing. She likes to look at the world through windows and windscreens: 'I love being on buses, I get great ideas on buses, just looking out the windows, getting snapshots of things as they pass by, anything that strikes me as exciting or interesting or even if it strikes me as intensely boring, if it is unusual in its intensity I write it down' (Norris, *Writers in Scotland*, p.2). Life is best looked at, not through a single window, as Nick Carraway suggests in *The Great Gatsby*, but through many windows. One thinks here of the shop windows in 'Fearless' and 'Need for Restraint', the way they function both to reflect and displace violence. The little girl who kicks back at the bully in 'Fearless' and the boyfriend who physically restrains the woman in 'Need for Restraint' are violent reactions to violence. Repression not only leads to violence but is itself a kind of violence.

Gifford's remarks on 'A Week with Uncle Felix' in particular bear examination, as they reveal the kind of masculine sensibility that Galloway works to undermine:

> The last and longest story, 'A Week with Uncle Felix', eschews the previous grotesquery and simply tells itself from the point of view of a young girl away for a week with her dead father's brother and his wife. Very little happens, apart from trips, teas, desultory chat, but Galloway captures the girl's isolated unhappiness perfectly along with the sadness of her uncle and his unsuccessful attempts to bridge the gap between them. (Gifford 1997, p.609)

In fact the dead father's brother's wife—June—is dead. The other woman, Grace, is Felix's sister, aunt to the young girl, Senga. But this is not the sole slip in Gifford's essay. Galloway's account of one of Uncle Felix's attempts to 'bridge the gap' is revealing:

> Don't cry, love. Don't.
> his lips parting as the breath slid out.
> Cry.
> Slipping.
> She was reaching out to him when something started slipping. Not the covers but a hand, his hand moving closer and beneath the quilt. He was looking down into her face and touching her through the nightie while her body locked, knowing and not knowing at the same time, letting the hand search over the chest to cup one breast.
> Give your uncle a kiss. Goodnight kiss.
> Goodnight kiss hissing like escaping gas. The cotton slid on her legs and the headboard rocked as he pulled closer, dipping the bed with shifting weight, the dry fingers on her skin. She knew she wouldn't shout. The headboard tipped the wall. Sudden and hard, the noise pulled the room too close, too real. The hand stopped, rested on her thigh through the cloth. Single strokes of the bedside clock getting louder. Then his voice, overhead.

It's all right, everything's all right, pet.
Almost a different voice. The quilt relaxed as he sighed. (pp. 175–6)

The 'strokes of the bedside clock' suggest a mechanical motion of another type. This is a horror story, a story of obsession and possession. The 'kiss hissing like escaping gas' conjures up images of a ghost rising from the grave. The word 'ghost' itself derives from the gas that emanates from a corpse in the process of decomposition. This painful encounter has been a long time coming. A week is a long time in the life of a young woman looking for her dead father in the eyes of her uncle, while he's looking for her mother in her eyes: 'But you know the really telling thing is the eyes. Never heard our Grace say it but your eyes are just your mum. Just Greta looking at you'. It emerges that her uncle's attitude to her mother, his sister-in-law, is ambiguous, a potent mix of attraction and repulsion:

Haven't seen your mum for too long, years and years. Could have had a good life, your mum. But kept too much to herself. Too proud to ask for help, wouldn't take it. Too bloody deep. I had a soft spot for your mum. Best legs in Scotland. And you're going to be just like her. Wanton little thing. (p. 176)

As well as coping with being her father's 'spit', an expression that sticks in Senga's throat, covering a multitude of sins, she has to contend with being her mother's too, and consequently with being a small object of desire for an amorous uncle.

From the moment she sets eyes on Uncle Felix, Senga sees someone who lives up to his name, a cat, a predator: 'Leopard-skin with shadow, the man crouched in the open door-frame. Uncle Felix'. (p. 131) His first words and actions, like his initial appearance, are heavy with insidious intent:

Out you come Sweetheart.
One shiny eye free of the patches of dark. It took a moment to realise who the Sweetheart was. Then whether it was a joke. He was holding out his hand.
Out you come. (p. 131)

The leopard never changes its spots once it has spotted its spit. Faced with its brother's spit, it puts pressure on its prey: emotional, psychological, physical. Showing her to her room, Felix again confuses roles and relations when he asks his niece: 'This all right, madam?' (p. 135) It is clear that Felix, the brother of a dead father of whom she has been told she is a mirror image, has a special place in Senga's young life, and in her memory. On her first morning, she hesitates, remembering that she must be dressed and decent before venturing out of her room: 'The bathroom downstairs and there being men about the place… Not just men: Uncle Felix'. (p. 136) 'Felix' comes from the Latin for 'fruitful', from an Indo-European base meaning 'to suck, suckle'. Its roots are wrapped up in 'felicity' and 'fellatio'. What Gifford calls 'the sadness of her uncle' is something more poignant and more painful, something which belies the felicitous aspect of his name.

Her uncle's feline nature is reinforced for Senga by his breakfast habits: 'Felix stood with his back to the sink, eating the substance of the fish smell from a blue plate … Felix smiled through hairy bones, dislodging something from between his back teeth'. (p. 137) That evening, Felix proposes a toast: 'To blood ties, he said. To us'. (p. 142) And like all the offerings in *Blood*, it is very much a question of blood ties, blood relations, and consanguinity. Several times, Senga—sanguine—senses that something is being implied that is just out of her reach. For example, discussing her father, Felix uses a gardening metaphor:

> You know who was the sweetpea man? Your dad liked the sweetpeas.
> He was the boy for the flowers all right. Green fingers.
> He blinked and shook his head.
> Sweetpeas and roses: that was your daddy. That was Jock all right.
> (p. 144)

The fact that Felix's wife, June, died 'pruning currant bushes' suggests that male fruit and female flowers are at odds. Prunes, of course, are dried plums, and plums play a crucial part in Felix's seduction of his brother's daughter.

Senga's first close encounter with the plums is a scene of temptation weighted with sin and significance. On her 'hunkers' in the garden, eyeing the fallen plums, she reaches out for one:

> Dark red, the skin loose and warm. It slipped when you touched, the flesh separate and firm underneath. Her finger left a dark shape of itself where it melted off the bloom. She opened her hand and picked up the whole fruit; thumb and first fingertip, end to end, lifting it nearer. Then

it became something else. Grey blue fungus furred one side of a gash underneath, a running sore oozing brown pulp and something else. Something moving. Thin black feelers twitching towards her hand. Dropping it was immediate. Even then it wasn't far enough away and she drew back from under the shade of the trees, staring, wiping her hands against the jean seams to get rid of the feel from her fingers. Black movements flickered at the corners of her eyes, everywhere now she looked. Ants. It was just ants. Ants couldn't do you any harm. The grass kept moving, wriggling under her feet. Shivering, she went inside for a cardigan. (p. 146)

Ants couldn't hurt you, but uncles could, especially uncles with overripe plums. Uncles, like carbuncles, could make you feel unclean. According to the *OED*, 'Uncle', as well as meaning brother of mother or father, can be a colloquialism denoting an 'unrelated man friend of children'.

In his niece's bedroom on her last night, Uncle Felix gives Senga something to remember him by, something she'll never forget. These are the pearls that were his eyes, 'unavoidable eyes coated with pale yellow film' (p. 175). The pearls he gives her are perilous: 'Three or four beads pattered onto the rug, pinholes staring up like tiny eyes' (p. 178). And there are plums to go with the pearls, family jewels of a different kind:

The skin of his cheek magnified, the depth of creases and thread-veins, unavoidable eyeballs coated with pale yellow film. And she realised he had meant what he said, asking her to remember this old man. And he was, he was an old man. Pictures of him at home were turning brown. Her father's brother. She might never see him again. (p. 175)

Felix leaves a ghastly impression on his niece. The story is a haunting memory of an impressionistic young woman stalked by her father's brother, and by extension, her father's ghost. Galloway is a writer of ghost stories— what else is *The Trick is to Keep Breathing* but, like Toni Morrison's *Beloved*, a tale of a haunting that follows a trauma, and, ultimately, an exorcism? When Felix leaves Senga's bedroom calling her 'sweetheart' again, a phantom touch remains: 'A ghost where his hand had been on her breast'. (p. 177) The farewell photograph of 'Felix and his niece, arm in arm' sustains the impression of lovers. (p. 179)

In fact, 'A Week with Uncle Felix' takes us back to 'Blood', and to the bruising, battering reality of male power over women, whether it be the brute force of the dentist, the cruel misogyny of the glaring graffiti, the woman-fearing student, or, as here, the abusive relative. Not just in the title tale, but all through the collection, men are exercising power at women's expense. Uncle Felix is, like Fearless, like the old man in 'Frostbite', like the restraining boyfriend in 'Need for Restraint', like the priest at Michael's funeral in *The Trick is to Keep Breathing*, like the doctors, like the uncommunicative and inexpressive Paul, an oppressor of women. What we find here are women keeping quiet for the sake of men, suffering in silence a violence whose voicing is more threatening to a damaged masculinity than its execution. But we also find women getting angry and getting even.

That anger is not to every reader's liking. Douglas Gifford sees in *Foreign Parts* a move away from the angry young woman of *The Trick is to Keep Breathing*: 'What is important in this novel is Galloway's dissipation of bitterness. The claustrophobic and deliberately unattractive aspects of *The Trick is to Keep Breathing*, arising from Joy's endless caricaturing of health visitors, doctors, teachers, and ministers, many of whom did indeed wish to help her, was accurate and unkind' (Gifford 1997, p.610). If it was accurate it wasn't caricaturing, and men being helpful can be a hindrance to women. Indeed, Gifford admits that the 'bitterness' has not entirely dissipated: 'There is a trace of the old asperity in Cassie's diatribes against men—who needs them?—and these can seem out of tune with the slow pace of movement through France, and through Cassie's exploration of herself. But Galloway places these angers in the context of Cassie's realization of the waste of human life in the Normandy graveyard, a perception which makes her look at her own life and frustration' (Gifford 1997, p.611). Gifford points out that Cassie's rage manifests itself in the face of the blithe language of tourism: 'It is easy to love ANGERS' (Gifford 1997, p.610).

According to Gifford, 'Galloway has a sympathy for both parties in male–female relations… which stands well back watching the game, letting the women's voices be heard as often querulous and irritating'. (Gifford 1997, p.611). Gifford gives the examples of 'Home' and 'While He Dreams of Pleasing His Mother' in *Where you find it*, as stories which present women in an unattractive light, but both tales could be read as representations of women produced by men—the restrained wife and the overbearing mother. Of *Where You Find It* Gifford concludes: 'Perhaps the most poignant of the group of stories is 'Baby-sitting', which tells of two wee boys ferreting in their father's pockets for money for fish suppers. Their squalid living conditions are seen—or not seen—from their point of view, as is their bewilderment about their father. Neither the brusque outsiders, the lady in the chip shop, nor the boys, know that the father is not dead' (Gifford 1997, p.612).

The lapse into Scots—'wee boys'—suggests warmth and an affinity missing from the previous commentary on the 'querulous and irritating' women. Wee boys will be bloody men, and bloody men will be wee boys. Fearless, Frostbite and Felix are wee boys. Wee boys bent on blood and butchery. Looking at her uncle's RAF photograph Senga hears her mother's voice, angry and compelling:

> Stupid uniforms, the war. A lot of men talking about planes and guns, things that had nothing to do with anything. Nothing important. *They're all the same, football and fighting and drink. Motorcars. Wee boys. Bloody men.* Then she was embarrassed, alone on the stairs and embarrassed as if somebody had heard it out loud. Her mother didn't know everything. Maybe a lot of men were like that but not Felix; opening doors and helping you in and out of the car. He washed the dishes and did shopping, gave you chocolates and ran the bath, called you pet, sweetheart, love. (p.172; emphasis in original)

The perfect boyfriend or husband, by the sound of it, except that he's her uncle, and anyway, in Galloway's fiction men may do the dishes, shop, buy chocolates, run baths, and open doors for women, but that doesn't free them from feminist critique. If men think the odd bit of housework—dishes are usually the limit—and a bribe or two can exonerate them, then they have another think coming. In fact, they're onto plums. Galloway has expressed doubt at the premature celebration of equality, pointing out that 'while differences have indeed been effected with regard to confidence, feasibility, acceptance and opportunity for women writers, it doesn't follow that everything is swimming' (Galloway, 'Introduction' to *Meantime*, p.4).

Where Gifford pathologises Joy by suggesting that she was externalising her guilt and blaming others, Galloway identifies guilt as gendered. Male abuse of power is the objective correlative: 'The need to keep women feeling guilty goes deep, obviously. The fear of losing the unfair system that operates in male favour likewise. It is still something for women to bear in mind, something to consciously resist' (Galloway, 'Introduction' to *Meantime*, p.7). Galloway has dipped her pen in gall, and used it to cauterise guilt.

Galloway makes it difficult for the helpful male critic to take up a position outside of the misogyny she identifies, which is not to say that all men are misogynists but that all men have to deal with their own inscription in male power relations. In *Blood*, 'Fearless' and 'Need for Restraint' are linked by the fact that the restrained and restraining boyfriend is no less culpable than the openly aggressive representative of impoverished masculinity. The body, sexual difference and subjectivity are three areas in which Galloway works closely. She gives us snatches of conversation that subvert spheres of influence, pearls secreted within plums.

Between the extraction at the root of *Blood* and Derek's dental kiss in *Where You Find It*, we have a series of injections, drillings, and fillings. Reading Galloway is at times like pulling teeth, or swallowing plums that still have stones lurking inside them. As Margery Metzstein says: 'Blood… becomes a powerful symbol in this story for those aspects of the female which cannot be contained and which cause fear, whether evinced as a patronising jocularity or a more marked revulsion, but most importantly force the female into a guilty paradox, on the one hand complicit with the ideology which equates woman with guilt, on the other resistant, yet unable to escape from its tentacles'. (p. 144) A kick in the tentacles, perhaps with a mule, or any she will do, may be one way of loosening the vice-like grip of male-induced guilt.

At the end of 'A Week with Uncle Felix', we are told that 'the stink of plums began rising from the boot, thickening behind sealed windows'. (p. 179) We are back with windows once again. Our first sight of the plums had been through a glass darkly:

> Plums. Attached to the ends of thin sticks where they were growing. Living things. There were more in the garden, dark shapes among the green when you looked … Plums right outside for heaven's sake. She rapped the glass with her knuckles and watched them shiver. (p. 142)

Shiver me plums, before they stink the boot out. Aunt Grace, we recall, had tried to do the job earlier, but only in a half-hearted fashion: 'The girl stretched, pulled at the neck of her shirt as Grace came back near the trench, kicking the bowls with the sides of her shoe'. (p. 151) This is trench warfare, but where Drake played with his bowls as the Armada approached, Grace shows Senga how to fight back, if only in a tangential fashion.

Duncan, meanwhile, is whistling 'Clementine', but what is lost and gone forever is not merely the innocence of an abused little girl, but the fruit of her father's loins, and her mother's labour. A clementine is a kind of fruit, small and round, but it is another fruit whose scent lingers at the story's end. The stink of plums rising from the boot is a fitting footnote to this essay, for Galloway's writing, like the little girl at the end of 'Fearless', kicks like a mule, and it is no shin-high affair. Galloway has an extra leg. She describes herself as 'female, working-class, Scottish. That's it. I have got three feet'. (Norris, p. 23) That gives her balance when she goes for the crux of the matter. This kick is powerful, and aimed at the plums, even at the very stones. The writing flows from blood to juice, and the kick inside is directed outward, towards the locus of power and authority. Plums are foreign parts, and the close of the novel of that name throws up a stone of its own:

> The stone. I hear it, the sound of solid matter ticking over an insupportable surface: faint blips and splashes. That the skin of water should be tough enough is a constant surprise. I turn to watch and can't help it. I cheer too. Another scuds out, headed for where Dunkirk might be, or home. It could be going home. Godknows. I've no sense of direction, me. I haven't a bloody clue. Rona and me. We stand in separate places, looking out over the water that is just water. Rona takes fresh aim, laughing. Defying gravity. (Galloway, *Foreign Parts*, p. 262)

This is writing that hits home hard, kicking and pruning with wild abandon.

Going all the way, Galloway plumbs the depths of female rage.

Works cited

Galloway, Janice (1989) *The Trick is to Keep Breathing*. Edinburgh: Polygon.
—— (1991) 'Introduction', *Meantime: Looking Forward to the Millennium, Women 2000*. Edinburgh: Polygon, pp. 1–8.
—— (1996) *Blood*. London: Minerva [1991].
—— (1995) *Foreign Parts*. London: Vintage [1994].
—— (1996) *Where You Find It*. London: Jonathan Cape.
Gifford, Douglas (1997) 'Janice Galloway', *A History of Scottish Women's Writing*, ed. Douglas Gifford and Dorothy McMillan, Edinburgh: Edinburgh University Press, pp. 607–12.
Norris, Fiona (1994) *Writers in Scotland*. London: Hodder and Stoughton.

Breaking through cracked mirrors
The short stories of Janice Galloway

Josiane Paccaud-Huguet

> It is language in excess of meaning, women in excess of any male
> determination, that produces the disease in the imaginary that narrative
> attempts to cure… if the reality of female sexuality threatens language,
> the narrative is concerned to smooth over this reality and to leave men
> and meanings uncontaminated by bodies or sounds. (MacCabe 1978)

Modernist narrative, as is well known, has thrown into the toilets the creams
and unguents which give classic realist texts their finely smoothed texture,
and chosen instead to expose in crude daylight the cracks of language and
human experience. Being a Scottish writer and a woman has endowed Janice
Galloway with a privileged insight into the reality of fragmentation which we
find both as a motif and a structuring principle in her collection of stories,
significantly entitled *Blood*. My aim here is to explore the modalities, taking
as a working hypothesis that the cast of characters, the places and events in
the different stories are variants on a pattern which I will in the last analysis
relate to the 'play of energy' underlying narrative desire. As the title story
suggests, the chief concern is about the loss of one's wholeness, with the fear
and violence of exclusion that it engenders in social and language codes.
What emerges here is a voice speaking from and of the dislocations of
womanhood, 'that sweet thorny place' (Toni Morrison): a voice that, like

Woolf, Joyce and Beckett, chooses to shatter the delusion of narrative as a mirror held up to nature. We are made to see that there is no such thing as nature out there waiting to be rendered by words, that gendered identity is an ideologically loaded construct. And we needn't after all be afraid to crack open the falsely protective shell of words or narrative, since what we encounter is the infinite chain of signifying forms and differential meanings. Instead of repressing the otherness of life and language, Galloway celebrates it in her playful experiment with form that reveals the tragedy of a universe left gaping over a core of darkness. In the drive among the wreckage, better to tear up playfully the plaster on the cracks than break through the wall and die hopeless like her figures of disinherited humanity.

Wasteland, crack-lines, and fear

In the fictional world of these stories, the desolation of landscapes—whether exterior or interior—signifies much more than the experience of local colour (contemporary life in Scotland) or 'feminine' perceptions—fields so far 'reserved' in the sense of Indian reservations, for female novelists. Galloway's texts speak to those who try to read the contemporary world through eyes no longer blindfolded; they invite us to leave the old befeathered ego in the closet and listen to the hidden determinants of subjective experience. If the typical image of modernist experience is 'the two-second encounter at some busy urban cross-roads' (Eagleton 1989, 21), Galloway (1991) completes the image in her own terms:

> …a straggling T-junction split the erratic paths of children and women following the grounds home with headscarves and late shopping (p. 32)

As one of her female narrators indicates, it is the private voices of women and children, so far unheard or covered by the traffic noise, which we are now made to hear.

Their world resembles Eliot's wasteland transposed to the postmodernist zone; a school which has no gate, 'just a gap in the wall with pillars' (p. 4), an old woman's flat with a scent of the grave, 'a faint cloy of earth and cold meat' (p. 48), photos of an aircraft shot down in 1944, lying among trees and smoke 'like a dinosaur carcass' (p. 153). A world of decomposition, therefore, of cracked mirrors which can no longer reflect the image of full subjects, where doors and windows *tear* open over the craters of experience. Last, but not least, a world devoid of any authoring or authorising truth:

> I stopped because there was no help for it and stood peering out at the visible sand, searching for what I couldn't see… Thinking there is something more I can make sense of, something more to come… There was still no answer. (p. 125)

The crack, however, opens not only in the topography of the city of the dead for which Glasgow seems to be a fit metaphor. It is also written in the fault-lines of human bodies, more particularly female bodies whose reality Joyce was the first writer to joyfully uncover: Galloway in her own bitterly witty way, reveals this body as the locus of projection for male fears. In the imaginary representations of these stories, the mouth with its threatening orality is the crack-in-the-face, loaded with connotations of loss and death. An old woman manages to make 'a slack oblong of her mouth with lips parted and some teeth showing in the divide' (p. 49) for a smile, before she swallows the pills that will lull her to eternal sleep. But it is in the title story, 'Blood', that the metaphor is more fully explored with its inherent sexual implications. From the outset the scene at the dentist's reads as a substitution for the sexual act, in terms of cruel domination. As the dentist triumphantly pulls a bloody lump out of the girl's creaking jaw, blood makes 'a pool under her tongue'. Symptomatically enough he gets rid of the problem by passing it on to his female assistant, who gives the girl a sanitary towel which she puts up blushingly to her mouth. She walks heroically back to school, unable to relieve herself since she knows that girls don't spit in the street.

A male rule with a textual revenge, however, since we are offered a lengthy description of the slimy pad in her mouth, of course reminiscent of Molly Bloom's concern with bodily flows of all sorts. It is no surprise to find that the blood from the cracked jaw metonymically heralds the other flow for which it is a metaphor. The churning in the girl's guts warns her that she will have to visit Mrs McNiven, the Cerberus of the senior girls' purgatory: instead of going there for *two* sanitary towels, however, she decides to use 'that horrible toilet paper'. The subsequent visit to the girls' toilets obviously reads as the female counterpart of the toilet scene in *Ulysses* (pp. 5–6). But this isn't the whole story: she wants to forget the miseries of her double loss by going upstairs to the music room where she will play something 'fresh and clean'. She plays so well that a female-shy cello student comes in, asking her to continue. As she is about to say 'it's Mozart', she feels her own blood welling up and spilling over the piano and floor. Fear and guilt follow as the student shuts the door hard behind him. Now we grasp the full bitterness of Mr Gregg's joke about the student, 'afraid of the girls and who could blame him haha' (p. 7). The student is the product of certain cultural habits whereby paternal advice consists in initiating a son into mistrust with the words 'Trust nae cunt' (p. 16).

The misogyny of cultural representations also lies at the core of another story, 'Fearless'. Fearless is a mythical figure who, in the citizens' eyes, embodies the unpredictability and arbitrariness, the *otherness* of life. We are told that like Marley's ghost he 'just appeared suddenly, shouting threats up the main streets' (p. 110) at people who just had to avert their eyes. On a symbolic level, Fearless is a figure of death who comes unexpectedly at you and won't bear being looked at. In the perspective of the community's imaginary representations, however, things take on a different shade: his disturbed state is ascribed to the fact that his wife left him—'After all, you had to remember his wife left him. It was all our fault really', the female narrator concludes (p. 113). None of the men therefore tries to calm down his angry invectives against women. One day he chooses the girl's mother as his victim: the girl wonders what it is that can be threatening, 'what did he think we were plotting, a woman and a wean in a pixie hat?' (p. 114). She looks back in anger, swings her foot at him, and he limps away. The allegorical value of the episode is disclosed at the end of the story:

> My mother is dead, and so, surely, is Fearless. But I still hear something like him: the chink and drag from the close-mouth in the dark, coming across open, derelict spaces at night, blustering at bus stops where I have to wait alone. With every other woman, though we're still slow to admit it, I hear it, still trying to lay down the rules. It's more insistent now because we're less ready to comply, look away and know our place. And I still see men smiling and ignoring it because they don't give a damn. They don't need to. It's not their battle. But it was ours and it still is…
>
> The outrage is still strong, and I kick like a mule. (p. 115).

As I will suggest later, writing is also for Galloway some sort of kicking at the Otherness congealed in the male-oriented representations of life and language.

The fear of division and loss, seen this time from a girl's perspective, is the motif of 'Into the roots' where the excessive, threatening flow is not menstrual blood but hair. Alice's first salon-cut induces in her a feeling 'as though her head were rising like a cork from the bottom of a sink of water' (p.59). A birth which is a separation from her 'still writhing' pleat as she gazes at someone else, her new solitary self, emerging in the mirror. What we have here is a playful rendering of the Lacanian mirror-stage in which the human subject meets the otherness of visual/verbal images that are the death of imaginary narcissism and the precondition for the entry into the symbolic order of language. The haircut also clearly reads as a castration, this time at the hands of the mother who then brews a distaste for the relic, the girl's 'precious matted *snake-in-the-box*' (p.60) which one day disappears. The cut, however, triggers 'fresh growth' (p.60) that makes people suspicious because they can't see Alice's eyes through the fringe—another excess, which again brings *penalties* on her (p.60). Years later we see her choking back her fear and plunging her hand into a tree hole full of the now recovered hair.

Looking in the face of Fearless Otherness, knowing that all you have to do is 'refuse to look scared and then nothing could touch you' (p.156), is a temptation represented in these stories in the form of the death-drive—a breaking through the wall—whose metaphorical equivalent will be the plunge through the cracked mirror of language and its representations.

Breaking through the wall

The passage from wasteland to voyeuristic breaking through into the world of fantasy is the motif of the story significantly entitled 'Breaking through'. Janet lives with her mother next to the cemetery wall and next to another flat occupied by an old woman, Bessie, and her cat, Blackie. Janet longs for the touch of Blackie's fur whose essence she wants to 'absorb', especially when the cat is on the rug, looking into the fire. The truth of the desire for the touch of death emerges in the shift from reality to what we assume to be fantasy—without any clear-cut textual line being drawn, however: one day Blackie falls into the fireplace and burns under the girl's eyes until the last that remains of him is 'a stink of scorched meat' (p.67). A few days later, as Blackie's old mistress thrusts herself forward into the flames, the girl lifts the poker to help her—a gesture of complicity which signifies that Blackie, then the old woman, function as projection spaces for her own desire.

The wall itself materialises in another story. An old couple choose to end their meaningless life by dashing their car into an unplastered brick wall fencing a derelict space where a steelworks used to be. The encounter with death is planned to take place at the end of the 'drive across the bridge and into the wasteland by the steelworks wall' (p. 106), the focus of a desire which takes the form of penetrating the cracks between the bricks:

Just bricks. Maybe they would plaster it over to make it look better later on… His hands felt dry, coated with dust, feeling for the absent plaster… (p. 104)

The crossing over into the underworld is the object of another fantasy in 'it was'. The stepping over the limits is suggested by the liminal time (nightfall) and place: the girl walks on a grass *verge* that neighbours the macadam 'to the *edge* of her vision' (my emphasis, p. 33). The trespassing is performed by a rite of passage, a sort of second death, and experience of mutilation wilfully controlled and therefore enjoyed as she kneels on the grass, 'overwhelmed… to feel the cling of the cool blades wrap the bare skin, exposed' (p. 33). Like D.H. Lawrence's artist figure in a similar experience—Gudrun in *Women in Love*—she is 'near to weeping with the pleasure of it… in panic at the foolishness of her joy' (p. 33).

We only need to follow the logic of the signifier which leaves the girl standing at a 'now grey privet hedge'—to be overheard as *private edge*—with the 'stubby hardness of cropped branches' hurting her hand. Her reaching into the underworld of death-in-life materialises with a sickly scent from underneath the edge, and something shiny under a drainpipe—the unnameable 'it'. As she digs up a face from the encroaching dirt and mud, the ontological shift from a real to a possible world occurs—'There was no need to acknowledge anything unusual in the situation for nothing was' (p. 34): a built-in comment on the form which the narrative then assumes, and to which I will return later. The girl is both fascinated and horrified at the friendly voice raised from the dead, inviting her into a lost world. She knows at the same time that Uncle George's ghost will live as long as she wills it—not only in the fantasy but also, the critical reader has to infer, in the subsequent narrative: a crucial metafictional comment on the artist's own death drive and fascination for de-composition, alongside his/her role as puppeteer which is the effect of the instinct for re-composition.

The metaphorical connection between the fascination with decomposition and the dark impulse at the core of the sexual drive is revealed from different angles in the various stories: the male perspective of repression

60

is crudely and cruelly suggested in 'the meat', an episode staged in a butcher's shop with, as central character, a carcass hanging from a claw hook, 'flayed and split down the spinal column' (p. 108), exposed for everybody's eyes and noses. The narrative centre of the story is occupied by the infectious process of putrefaction, until the butcher slices the thing down and throws it to the dogs. The next morning he recovers the remains: he seals the hair and a piece of tartan ribbon in 'a plain wooden box beneath the marital bed'—a diminutive coffin for a wife butchered—and perhaps also for Scotland murdered, the reader reflects in a chilling retrospective black flash.

The analogy in war between nations and between the sexes is pursued in the long, powerfully symbolic story 'A week with Uncle Felix', with a female perspective this time. As Senga looks hard at the picture of a plane's carcass dripping 'wreckage like rotten meat' (p. 153), she uncurls her hand from the coins in her pocket, her palm smelling of 'stale metal'. The gesture is the narrative transposition of the unconscious textual connection between wrecked carcass and female body, the very structuring principle of 'the meat'. Senga's impulse, here, is not to slice down and hide, but to follow the bent of her fascination/repulsion for the living things underneath the crack/wound, through the metaphor of the rotting plums:

> …That thick sweet smell like metal… rotten fruit. It lay and rotted and sugars came and something else, she forgot what… wanting to look closer, she… reached for the nearest… Dark red, the skin loose and warm. It slipped when you touched, the flesh separate and firmer underneath. Her finger left a dark shape of itself where it melted off the bloom… Grey blue fungus furred one side of a gash underneath, a running sore oozing brown pulp and something else. Something moving. Thick black feelers twitching towards her hand… Black movements flickered at the corner of her eyes… Ants… The grass kept moving, wriggling under her feet. (p. 146)

It is of course not accidental that the scene takes place in her dead aunt's garden with its crew-cut green and 'rose bushes pruned back to stumps' (p. 151), or that she then offers herself a private joke by buying nail varnish whose name is 'Sugar Plum'. What is suggested here is that the initiation into the knowledge of death is concomitant of the discovery of sexuality, since both entail separation from imaginary wholeness and initiation into the reality of *difference*: the remarkably consistent network of metaphors in

Galloway's stories suggests that it is the narcissistic wound resulting from that separation which contaminates the gender relations.

Il n'y a pas de rapports sexuels

Jacques Lacan's famous provocation—'there is no such thing as sexual intercourse'—might serve as a comment on the unbridgeable fault-line in Galloway's representation of gender relations, a fault-line in turn dividing the very language of these texts, introducing us to the impossibility of smooth textual relationships, since language is the symbolic locus of difference.

For Senga in 'A week with Uncle Felix', the initial experience of loss originates in a double betrayal, the death of her father with the inherent loss in language representations, alongside her mother's invectives against the other sex. Like her fictional sister in 'Frostbite' who looks vainly about in search of a 'man who would be shamed by her struggling on her own' (p. 20), Senga is a figure of orphaned childhood—'Dad. The *word* never felt right', she muses (my emphasis, p. 165). The only thing she wants to ask from her dad's brother, Felix, is 'What was his spit?', an arrestingly ambiguous sentence meaning 'What did he look like?', but also pointing to the threatening, phallic connotations of 'spit'—a spike, a 'thin pointed rod for sticking meat onto and turning over for cooking over a fire' (Longman dictionary). We needn't go too far to find a confirmation of this second reading: during the week Senga has been to the local museum where, along with the war photos, her attention focused on some farming tools. Now farming—husbandry—is a common enough metaphor for the sexual act since it is the tracing of lines and opening 'cracks' in the mother earth. Among the tools she sees a bridle with a flat iron *spike* for the horse's mouth, with a telling joke on the card next to it: 'For wives who scolded or told lies' (p. 153).

Senga's question, therefore, is double-edged: it involves curiosity about one's origin, and sexual curiosity as well. We shouldn't be too surprised to read that Senga 'suddenly suspected the answer' about her father's spit, that 'It was something too terrible to know about' (p. 176). Once more she is punished for her curiosity when she is given the answer: in her dad's words, 'obligingly' quoted by Uncle Felix, she was 'a mistake… But jus fun' (p. 176): a confirmation that her existence was neither authored not authorised, and a warning about her place in gender positions.

It is inscribed within the unconscious logic of the text that she should then become her uncle's sexual toy: before he tries to abuse her, he gives her his dead wife's string of beads on faded red velvet—an obvious sexual symbol— as sweat (another bodily flow) *beads* under her arms. The scene closes on the remark that she is going to be a 'wanton little thing' just like her mother. What is at stake here is male denial and projection in the face of the reality of the crack torn open by death and sexual difference: as is always the case, it is all women's *fault* in all the senses of the word. The implacable logic runs on, since she is offered a box of stinking plums as a farewell gift (p. 179).

Thus the latent equation rottenness/sexuality/guilt in a male-dominated world is the female inheritance in a story where 'It was all my fault' returns like a leitmotiv. Uncle Felix's house is a place of man smells—the 'salty smell of socks' (p. 155), 'a thickness of sauce and spice' (p. 133)—where Senga is 'shared' by the men of the household. She also discovers in their magazines images of female sexuality as *seen by men*—painted nails, make up, huge breasts—alongside the reality of her own body: as the forbidden pages tear open between her fingers, she breaks sweat. The consistency of the symbolic imagery suggests that her trespassing into her dead aunt's garden and into her uncle's room as well as the guilt, are sexual and determine the pattern of her further actions: as she opens her bedroom window, the frame cracks and she is stung by a wasp from the plum trees. Her finger now looks 'curled like a claw' and she feels punished for her curiosity: she shouldn't have torn open the magazine/cracked open the window/been too curious about her father's spit.

In the economy of gender relations, the loss which is supposed to be on the side of womanhood is that which authorises the existence of its opposite equivalent, i.e. male narcissism—a recurrent trait in the stories. Self-sufficiency, wholeness are figured by Tony who looks 'good, assured, masculine… relaxed in his ownership of the place' (p. 118). In 'Bikers', Big Jim 'radiates cleanliness' (p. 78) and the conversation between bikers is a fine example of myth-making which authorises the passage from 'wee boy' to grown man. Just like Barthes' DS in *Mythologies*, the bike is the domesticated divinity which confirms phallic power. The conversation is

…a ritual by heart: components of tea-ceremony, delicacy for Zen
brothers in black leather robes… Their minds will be clean, prayers for
gods that will one day run smooth as silk, purr like kittens, run like
dreams. (p. 79–81)

As can be expected, the complementary subjective position is the misogyny in the politics of language and cultural representations, whose aim is to repress the destabilising otherness.

Men, in the world of Galloway's stories, want neither to see nor to hear. Symptomatically, the dentist shows all his *fillings* when he grins at his spectacles, which he wipes with a cloth while his assistant gives the sanitary towel to the bleeding girl. Lack of empathy tainted with sadistic pleasure are latent in his 'Sandra'll get you something to stop making a mess of yourself' (p. 3). The student who used to pretend that he couldn't see girls when he went by them on the stairs, glances at the blood flow and shuts the door hard. In the story ironically entitled 'Need for restraint', a girl who protests against street violence and people 'practising mass avoidance' (p. 82), is silenced by her male companion's imperious 'Nothing to do with you'. She feels 'clumsy, inept, female... at fault somehow' (p. 89); the words jam in her mouth, as for her counterpart in 'Nightdriving':

> I opened the door shouting I'M COMING TOO... but the wind blotted up in my mouth and I knew there would be no answer. There would be no answer because I couldn't be heard. (p. 124)

The power of the word, instead, lies in the force of repression exemplified by the bleeding man's words of thanks to the girl who rescued him—'Keep away from bastart women, that's what yi do' (p. 28), by the sexist jokes—the dentist's 'Redheads bleed worse than other folks haha' (p. 3), or the 'fatuous and obscene things some men assumed a lassie carrying a violin case was asking for' (p. 27). Notwithstanding the animal metaphors for calling girls, 'hen' at best, 'cow' at worst. The sexist felt-tip drawings on the girls' toilet door in 'Blood' are accompanied by the comment in block letters, 'girls are a bunch of cunts' (p. 6) which leaves the poor girl ashamed and helpless.

It is the very possibility of relating the genders that is foredoomed in these stories: a one-night lover's kiss stretches a girl's lip 'till it splits' (p. 38). In 'Blood' the '*tearing* sound of the doorseals' seizes her stomach as the cello student comes to her (p. 8). The bloodflow in her mouth dooms to failure the only chance she is given to speak: no better metaphor could have been penned about the disease in the imaginary produced by 'language in excess of meaning, women in excess of any male determination' (MacCabe 1978), which in turn calls for the threat of castration both at the hands of men, and women—in 'Into the Roots', we are told that Alice's hair had always been excessive, that her mother 'tore out the knots and condemned them, spitting, to the flames. The longer it got, the more wayward it became' until one day 'enough was enough' (p.59).

Alice's resistance to the dominant prescriptions is signified by the fact that she won't take part in the 'tedious chants of births, marriages, turns-up-for-the-books' her mother wants to inscribe her in. Instead she becomes a scandal herself when she moves in with a man and lives 'in sin'. She reverses that which had been imposed on her when she promises herself a haircut for the week when she breaks with him—'butcher the whole lot short because he had liked it long' (p.61). The haircut with a revenge is a fictional representation of the pattern of repetition-with-reversal which, as I will try to demonstrate, is the very nerve of narrative desire: the choice in narrative strategies will be to peel the paper from the walls, leaving the cracks and craters exposed, like the narrator of 'Plastering the cracks' (p.90).

Speaking out from a place of one's own

The beginnings of the writer's gesture of response stems from the reversal of perspectives, the choice to speak from the locus of women. The narrator-focaliser in 'Frostbite' finds herself the unwilling addressee of the bleeding man's narrative.

> A man's story about what he would call *a bad woman*, and he would tell it as though she wasn't a woman herself, as though she shared his terms. As though his were the only terms (p.20)

The first person narrator of 'Fearless' steps in resolutely with her own terms:

> …women shouted their weans in at night with HERE'S FEARLESS COMING… weans made caricatures… and men? I have to be careful here. I belonged to the world of women and children on two counts, so I never had access to their private thoughts voiced in private places: the bookie's, the barber's, the pub… Maybe they said things in there I have no conception of. (p.112)

What we should be wary of in our turn is the fallacy of pseudo-omniscient viewpoints in 'realist' narratives, with their falsely totalising vision of truth. The vantage point of first person narration will provide a different focus on the private places from which women speak—for example the girls' toilets. Just as Senga stretches in her bedsheets 'to use up all the space deliberately' (p. 136), similarly her creator uses up all the narrative space allotted by the sheet of paper. The language of these stories is far from something 'fresh and clean' to make us forget the discourse of the body: it sounds more like 'the low echo coming through the wall' to which Senga enjoys listening, 'rocking on two legs with her eyes closed' (p. 107): it is not 'communication' between full subjects, therefore, but something like the sign language through the bedroom wall of 'Plastering the cracks'.

Along similar lines, narrative becomes a symbolic 'room' and place of one's own, both for Galloway's personified narrators and, at a second remove, for their creator. 'Nightdriving' is an allegory about the empty darkness of the postmodernist landscape where no one answers, where a young woman goes out to listen to the music swelling up in the night, where the only thing to do is keep driving on treacherous and twisting roads, steep 'like the sides of a coffin', among the 'husks of broken cars' (p. 127). Driving—like commanding a ship for Conrad's narrators in the heart of darkness—is an apt metaphor for authoring narrative and authorising significance, even though it now has to be among the rubble of modern civilisation. It is highly symbolic of course that the girl in 'Blood' tries to focus past the dentist's knuckles to the cracked ceiling, and to patch the lines up into some recognised pattern:

> She was trying to see a pattern, make the lines into something she could recognize, when her mouth started to do something she hadn't given it permission for. (p. 1)

What is that 'something she hadn't given it permission for', if not the necessary and impossible articulation of otherness in discourse which always *exceeds* the speaker's intention, so wittily figured by the blood in her mouth?

The absurdist fantasy of 'it was' should be read as an attempt, both in the language and in the representation, to give a shape to that which exceeds symbolisation, i.e. the Lacanian Real that by definition recedes into formlessness as soon as it is 'named'—hence the textual resistance, the blanks and fractures in the text. Like the young woman in 'Plastering the cracks', the narrator sets herself the task of re-opening the cracks and digging out 'it', a buried face revived from the dead. She operates delicately with her finger—

like the novelist careful to crack open the shell of words and sentences—as 'the silt crumbled and parted fairly dryly to slide out of the cracks it had claimed' (p.34). The figure raised from the dead, therefore, is literally the object of its creator's desire—'He had no awareness that he was dead and she would not let him know... She knew he wouldn't live far away' (p.35). What the fantasy represents is that the existence of 'it' is authored by narrative desire—a desire for mastery/authority over a lost object that eludes one's grasp in an indefinite metonymy.

We now need to return in more detail to 'Blood' in which, emblematically again, two modes of subjective position are figured: as repression of the truth about loss—'the mortal hole at the centre of the mother of all life' (Sibony 1982), and as wilful exposition, and therefore temporary mastery. What is foremost is that these two modes are correlative of two radically opposed politics of language and representation: on one hand, the 'realist', neurotically controlled mode: on the other hand, the modernist modes which choose to reveal the gap, alongside the ideological truths inherent in language choices. The lost tooth, with a strangely twisted root extracted from the cracked jaw, speaks about the reality of loss and its correlate, guilt:

> It had a ridge about a third of the way down, where the glaze of enamel stopped. Below it, the roots were huge... The twist was huge, still bloody where they [the roots] crossed... Hard to accept her body had grown this thing. Ivory. (p.7)

I wish to draw attention here to two key signifiers, 'enamel' and 'ivory'. As she begins to play the piano, the girl places the tooth near the keyboard: the scenic and textual contiguity between the tooth and the keys suggests the *metonymic* connection between loss and artistic production/symbolisation, since piano keys are made from ivory, i.e. elephant 'teeth'.

But this isn't the whole story: the episode provides a crucial insight into the relationship between language production and repression. This connection is made by means of the textual/semantic ellipsis, literally covered by the flow of words:

> It's Mozart—before she remembered.

> Welling up behind the lower teeth, across her lips as she tilted forward to keep it off her clothes. Spilling over the white keys and dripping onto the

clean tile floor. She saw his face change, the glance flick to the claw roots… (p. 8)

What is textually missing here is of course the repressed word, i.e. 'Blood', which should be the grammatical subject of 'welling up' and 'spilling over'. At the same time, the hole left by the missing signifier is *filled* by words in a way that is truly iconic of the necessary repression of loss, preliminary to the emergence of narrative. This is where the 'neurotic' mode fits in, as the textual correlate of the girl's attempt at 'patching something together and pretending one doesn't bleed'—'You could get past things that way, pretend they weren't there', she concludes, as she tries to 'be something else: a piece of music' (p. 8). What is implicit here is a conception of art/writing/music as a social alibi for repressing one's and others' bodily fears. Galloway, however, is determined to strip the plaster and reveal the cracks.

The narrative contiguity between the enamel of the tooth, the ivory of the keys and the *unstoppable* blood flow, is suggestive of what underlies cultural productions: underneath the fine arts/culture, lies the butchered elephant's blood, whose remains have been aestheticised into ivory keys. Similarly, the feminine body in 'Blood' is revealed as a suffering body under the varnish of civilisation, the locus of repression in which cultural productions are rooted. The guilt and shame, as is well known, are the victim's reward:

> They would be here before she could do anything, sitting dumb on the piano stool, not able to move, not able to breathe, and this blood streaking over the keys, silting the action… The unstoppable redness seeping through the fingers at her open mouth. (p. 8)

The logic of Galloway's writing, it now appears clearly, stems from a desire to render the underlying experience of fragmentation and, just like Joyce, to restore the reality of the female body with its holes and losses. What is foremost, however, is that the episode makes metaphorical a *structural* issue which goes far beyond the scope of a narrowly 'feminist' reading: what is at stake here is the truth of *difference*—in gender, race, nationality, age—and the return of the repressed from which cultural productions and layers of 'protective' language are nurtured. The functional analogy between the elephant tusk and the girl's tooth suggests that the companion text to 'Blood' might well be 'Heart of Darkness'. The artistic utterance of Janice Galloway in its turn proceeds from dumbness, from the unstoppable bloodflow to the inkflow seeping through the artist's fingers and from her open mouth—a truly illuminating insight into the urge and urgency of writing.

The excess of meaning in human bodies and in language is no longer covered but on the contrary exposed. In these stories the purpose of ordinary conversation seems to be to plaster the cracks of experience, like the pain of loneliness for the old woman at the moment of the health-visitor's leaving— 'Someone increases the volume further. We begin to appreciate the artistry of the health-visitor in this professional and crafted leavetaking' (p. 48). Such artistry and craft in language choices is of course irrelevant to Galloway's own art, which chooses to shatter the *falsely* protective layer producing the 'pretty fictions' (Conrad) of bourgeois realism. It is surely no accident if one of the rare examples of positive relationships in these stories occurs between a female narrator and the man 'with some terrible speech defect' whom she has hired to plaster the cracks in her bedroom:

> I hadn't been able to hear him right. No, that wasn't it. I had heard perfectly well. It was more that I didn't seem able to get to the bottom of what he was saying. I couldn't work out a meaning. It reminded me of a habit I had got into as a child... on long bus journeys. I would let the engine noise sink me into a kind of hypnosis till the sound lost its significance. Then when people spoke their words became simply noise, disembodied from sense... conversation became at once incomprehensibly foreign and deeply soothing: threatless music to block out exteriors. I encouraged it. But when it began to affect me unbidden I was frightened and stopped practice by sheer effort of will. (p. 95)

Words stripped of communication purposes, then, become 'deeply soothing', 'threatless music', by a practice of wilful exile that is preliminary to the novelistic impulse, itself an impulse toward mastery of the flow—symbolic this time.

It is in 'Into the roots' that the structure of narrative desire is best illustrated. At some point in her maturation as grown-up, Alice decides to remain on the brink of the flow of life from now on:

> She stopped walking... [and] trying to make up lost ground... Relief rubbed into her shoulders... warming affection for the disappearing figures ahead. Let them go... Alice stood and watched the familiar backs retreat as in a mirror. (p. 61)

This subjective position, I would suggest, symbolises the artist's exile and working on the fault-line between the living and the dead. Alice then moves towards a broken tree split and blasted to the sky, towards

> ... an eyesocket of a hole, with a swollen lip of bark and moss that only made the wound seem more raw. It would hurt, but had to be done... Choking back her fear, Alice thrust out and plunged two clawed fingers into the hole it was full of hair. (p. 63)

The clawed fingers, of course, duplicate the form of the dentist's pliers and the hairdresser's scissors. The gesture is literally a repetition with a revenge of these 'castrations' of which she is now the agent, no longer the sufferer, and which allow her to recuperate the lost hair/her. What is also figured here is the creator's headlong plunge into the split/black mouth/crack.

One important aspect of Galloway's politics of writing is her response to the dominant positions in language and representations. The little girl whose mother is attacked by Fearless feels the violence of language, the pressure of the 'loud, jaggy words which came out of the black hole of his mouth' (p. 114) even though she doesn't know the meaning. What matters is that when she dares turn and look at Fearless he stares back, and then 'the words had stopped' (p. 114). What is clearly suggested here is that the response consists in looking back in anger and speaking out, making oneself heard with a revenge for those who couldn't be heard before.

Il n'y a pas de rapports textuels: fractured form

Galloway's politics of writing bears the symptoms of the discontents of our civilisation, for reasons that Terry Eagleton expounds in an essay entitled 'Modernism, Myth and Monopoly Capitalism':

> .... the ways that liberal humanism defined the human subject... just aren't working any more... Fewer and fewer people.... can see themselves as the autonomous, sharply separate, strenuously self-regulating agents of their own historical destiny, whatever might have been possible for Walter Scott. Fewer people, too, can trust in the essential readability and intelligibility of the object, which is now typified by the opaque, fragmentary, impenetrable commodity. And nobody can muster much

faith any more in progress and historicity—modernism belongs with an epochal progress and historicity—modernism belongs with an epochal shift in our notions of temporality, with a refusal to believe that the world is any longer story-shaped, that it has an immanent causal logic which art has then only to represent… Modernism as a movement cuts indifferently across cities, societies, art-forms, languages, national traditions. Released from the Oedipal constraints of a motherland, it was able, from the vantage-point of some polyglot metropolis, to cast a cold eye on all such national heritages. (Eagleton 1989, pp. 22–3)

Hence, I would suggest, the resurgence of a Scottish modernism such as practised by Alasdair Gray, James Kelman and Janice Galloway: it is literally ground-breaking, and set up against the ideologically loaded forms nurtured by bourgeois narrative which is still alive and well in the British 'motherland'. But of course the questions that modernism raises are structural: simply the thickness and resistance of the plaster varies according to many parameters. As I already hinted, it is the stripping of the plaster that is at the core of Galloway's artistic concerns.

It will be no surprise to find that many of the stories are third-person narration with internal focalisation into, and from, a girl's now-transparent mind which becomes a fragmented locus of causal, perceptual and mental consciousness. The composition of 'Blood' indicates that Galloway has fully integrated the heritage of Woolf and Joyce: the rending/rendering of consciousness is Woolf's, whereas the 'obscenity' is Joyce's. We move from Bloom's voice (interior monologue) to the represented thought of a mind sifting the discourses of others, Galloway fully exploits the possibilities offered by the technique of Free Indirect Discourse by embedding male discourses within a female focalising conscience—thus she provides an alternative to the man-centred version about a 'bad woman' in 'Frostbite'. Her female focalisers are Molly Bloom's late-twentieth century companions, with an equal concern for the bloodflow, to which must be added a narrating voice's will-to-mastery over its metaphorical substitute, the inkflow.

The other dominant narrative mode in the stories is retrospective first-person narration, with the classic split between naïve experiencer and now-all-knowing narrator figure, resolutely and consistently female, wilfully playing on the game of imaginary identifications. 'Two fragments' is a craftily arranged piece where, again, the theme repeats the structure: it is a story *about* two fragments—granny's lost eye and a father's lost half-fingers— itself fragmented into two levels, a framing narrative and a framed story. In the embedded story the first-person narrator, a grown woman, becomes a 'you', the little girl listening to her mother's comic and dreadful tales of castration/ mutilation. What is worthy of note is that these tales are presented as female alternative *fictions* covering the grim truth of facts exposed in two lines: the father lost his finger in the army, the grandmother's eye was taken away by the explosion of impure coal 'given' to the miners' families by the coal board. Now it is the mother's bitter voice that is heard through the daughter's in a fiction wilfully subverting the factual truth in order to suit a child's want (p. 40)—pointing therefore at the very truth of narrative desire. In the mother's narrative the black threatening mouth is no longer any woman's fault, but the father's on two accounts: first because he drinks his pay— therefore his family's living—and secondly because his two missing half- fingers are the result of his own greed: one night he was so hungry that he ate his own fingers for chips with salt and vinegar (p. 40). It is no longer here a question of smoothing the excess in women's bodies, but the truth of the harsh realities—war, British colonialism, poverty. Thus, the tale ends with the grim nursery rhyme lines

> Fingers for the army
> An eye for the coal board
> A song and a dance for the wean. (p. 45)

Thus the force of narrative desire still aims to soothe the cracks of experience, but this time not for the dominant class, or gender.

It is the consolation of narration as unifying process that is also the structuring principle, the driving force of the three unrelated fragments of 'Nightdriving', in the absence of unity of time, space and character or of voice consistency. Elsewhere this force disintegrates in favour of merely scenic presentation in the pieces entitled 'Scenes from the life No...', symptomatically in jumbled order: No. 23, 29, 26, 24, 27. What is worthy of interest here is the focus on the fictional narratee as perceiver/voyeur/ participant and, to a certain extent, creator—therefore never innocent. The scenes are infused with topographical references that metaphorise the range of subjective positions for the implied reader, overtly determined by narrative manipulations. We are also meant to note scents or sounds, to advance on the stage and to return to our vantage point (p. 53), to doze when we are not interested, to afford 'a little sentimental soft-focus' (p. 54): we are even asked to wonder when we should break in or leave, to name a character now that it has become substantial enough (p. 55), or to question its paper substance—'It is difficult to discern where paper stops and flesh begins' (p. 56).

The narrative intention and design, therefore, is to defamiliarise the reader by shattering the nicely polished surface of narrative. The same strategy can be found in the language of these texts: one of the favourite devices is the foregrounded use of thematisation in the opening sentences of the stories, producing the effect of our entering a world already constituted—from which we are therefore alienated from the outset. In true post-modernist manner, Galloway also explores and subverts the potentialities of genre language and typography. 'Fair Ellen and the wanderer returned' is a subverted ballad, re-written from the perspective of a female focaliser. All the clichés are there, the man at the centre of the woman's vision, the 'we need never be separated again', but they are systematically deconstructed. As is the case with the Ballad of the Croppy Boy in *Ulysses*, it is not the sentimentalising voice of the good people that we hear, but a voice 'full of splinters' revealing the dullness of the waiting years and the drudgery of a late marriage of reason in the beloved's absence. When the wanderer returns the now grey-haired Ellen holds him in a 'long, black look' (p. 74), and her own narrative cuts 'through his words like a knife across meat' which takes away 'his right for self-pity' (p. 75). Similarly, I would suggest, Galloway's narratives cut through words and sentences to reveal the ideological substance of gender positions in the cultural codes.

Elsewhere the reader is taken to the cutting edge of the word and to the private edge of subjectivity in ways which are reminiscent again of Joyce or Beckett. Thus Galloway is able to exploit the polysemy and resonances of the most insignificant word—like 'it' in 'it was'. The story is built around the structurally doomed attempt to give a name and a shape to the nameless thing, to death and loss. The syntagm 'it was' decomposes into separate units, combines into new ones, radiates into different semantic fields according to its textual position, which symptomatically resists reproduction for the purposes of the present essay, because of the blanks and typography. The 'it' then substantialises into a cast character, a loving figure of the past—Uncle George, who now 'lives' in the girl's fantasy. The typography, which is here an essential element of significance, functions as a reminder that signifieds are not things out there, but forms—even though empty ones like the blank spaces which create an essential semantic void: the repetitions and the blankness are more significant than the 'it'. Thus we are made to see the 'it-ness' of that most neutral word in the language, the empty repository of many cultural representations—the most sensational being the Freudian 'it' which is not alien to the episode here.

The opposite equivalent of the blank is the defamiliarised use of the capital letters that invade and occupy the textual space in a way which metaphorically duplicates the violent force of male voices overheard by a girl at the bus-stop:

> dancin boys DANcin so we jist looks right then he's ach moan up the DANcin and fuckin away so we FOLLOWS him right we FOLLOWS him aff the bus up the STAIRS man these STAIRS fuckin STAIRS to the hoose fourth fuckin flair christ and in the lobby right and he STARTS right he STARTS wi this WEAN fucking wean in the livin room sittin this lassie christ pickin her up fuckin PICKIN her up… (p. 30)

What is foremost here is that the textual arrangement of the block letters makes up a sort of sub-text with its own patterns and formal repetitions which are in their turn the sign of the female focaliser's appropriation and re-inscription of the boys' discourse. It is no surprise either to find that Galloway's representation of discourse follows the now classic Joycean tradition which consists in rejecting inverted commas: 'perverted commas' (Joyce), since they are ideologically loaded markers of hierarchy and control in the representation of others' discourse: besides their presence, by fostering the illusion of voices quoted from the life, masks the homogenising force of narrative. The narrative form of Galloway's stories, once more, is homogenisation with a revenge since now it is the male voices that are digested into the melting pot of narrative, with some symptomatic points of resistance like the Scottish idiom.

A certain nostalgia for full meanings among some critical schools will have it that fragmented form is 'meaningless'. It is, in the sense that modernist/post-modernist modes of writing do not nurture their readers with stable truths or rounded character pattern in the way of the 'Victorian melodrama…Hearts and Flowers' which the girl in 'Frostbite' finds herself parodying (p. 26). I would suggest for my part that Galloway's writing is an outstanding example of living, ever-changing *significance*. It is neither minimalist verse, nor over-transparent language, two 'excesses' represented by the modes of the bikers' conversations:

> They chant in minimalist verses, machine-shop precise to make pattern

of tappets and points and overheated coils… BIG JIM seems to have paused for thought while our attention has been elsewhere and the mood has altered. His brow has darkened and when he speaks now it is no longer poetry: it is far too comprehensible. (p. 79)

Galloway's prose, in its turn, will have its own cutting edge, making us see and hear words that are like 'a tearing sheet', drawing attention to their power to *signify* rather than mean in a conclusive manner. The circular form of the long short story 'A week with Uncle Felix' is in this respect significant: here are the opening and closing sentences:

'Clementine'
The buzzing came clearer by degrees.

Duncan humming through the engine noise, the same bit over and over. (p. 130)

Duncan started whistling 'Clementine' as the stink of plums began rising from the boot… (p. 179)

As is usual in modernist narrative the circularity in form is symptomatic of the *absence* of conclusive meaning and answer. On the other hand the recurrence of the signifier 'buzzing' in two crucial episodes suggests the relation between narrative form and the black silence at the core of the girl's initiation into sexuality and death—'They said nothing about her father… The turntable started buzzing.' (p. 150). Language has lost its protective layer here, it reveals nothing but loss and absence. The narrative in places becomes like the turntable, but with many unheard tunes and unexpected sounds for the reader/listener's relish.

The similes and metaphors open an unconventional field of predominantly feminine, or domestic experiences: the painted borders of windows flake 'like late-in-the-day eye-liner' (p. 32): fair Ellen stands 'stiff as an ironing board' (p. 71): the claw root of the tooth is 'like a deformed parsnip' (p. 2), hair strays out fuzzily 'as though [she] had been plugged into an electric socket' (p. 59), a haircut reveals a long neck that 'had grown up in the dark like a silent mushroom' (p. 59).

The musical composition is overheard in the play of alliterations and assonances that make the text resonate with harmonics—'the cold tap spat water' (p.6): 'scented stock wafted up sickly from underneath it' (p.33), 'goodnight kiss hissing like escaping gas' (p.176), among many others. It is of course symptomatic that the musical patterns are better heard in non-referential passages as if the singing sounds were meant to be a consolation for the loss of referent. If we come close to poetry at times, the genre remains story-telling none the less, resolutely self-reflexive, baring its own devices—among these being the two founding principles of narrative, metonymy and repetition.

An apparently anodyne sentence like the following is rich in metafictional implications:

> Two-storey council terraces with frames of paint borders round the windows, flaking like late-in-the-day eye-*liner*, *lined* the opposite side of the road: (my emphasis, p.32)

It is the slightly modified repetition 'liner'/'lined' which gives here the text the energy to run on after the pause signified by the comma. It is also a telltale example of the fact that meaning proceeds by resemblances and differences (we move from noun to verb, from one sound/graphic pattern to another close form), that it is fabricated by metonymic contiguity—i.e. syntagmatic development along the *line* of narrative. Thus we shift in a self-reflexive movement from eye-liner to line of house, to line in the text: another illuminating example that a signified must always have been a signifier before it becomes a signified.

Not only do Galloway's texts point to the process of metonymy at work, but also they rely on metonymy as a working principle in the generation of significance, especially in places where the meaning resists as in the following passage:

> His hands felt dry, coated with dust, feeling for the absent plaster... on the way back he noticed the petrol light, orange dot on the *dash*board as he was approaching the *wall*... Then, for no reason he could think of, he remembered the *book*... He watched the *wall* in the rear-view mirror. (my emphasis, pp.104–5)

It is the textual contiguity between 'dashboard', 'wall' and 'book' that makes the reader suddenly grasp that the old man has found by an unconscious association the mode of his intended suicide—dashing his car into the steelworks wall—described in a biography of Arthur Koestler borrowed from the library. It is only in the light of these *textual* connections that this otherwise obscure piece of narrative can make sense.

I focused earlier on the crucial metonymic connection between the ivory of the tooth and of the piano keys, itself metaphorical of the relation of cause and effect between loss and creation. The passage is worth considering again from the angle of the metonymic connections it establishes and denies at the same time, as if the cultural unconscious were trying to cover its own tracks:

> The tooth... It had a ridge about a third of the way down, where the glaze of *enamel* stopped... *Ivory*. She smiled and laid it aside on the wood slate at the side of the *key*board, like a misplaced piece of inlay. It didn't match. The *keys* were whiter. (my emphasis, p. 8)

Galloway's artful craftswomanship is at its best here: on one hand the passage establishes the crucial unconscious connection enamel/ivory/keyboard/keys, whose *key* function in the process of significance is playfully signalled by the very redundancy of the word. On the other hand the text seems as it were to divert us from that connection by a double denial ('misplaced', 'it didn't match') which, I would suggest, is a perfect example of the Freudian negation which consists in saying the contrary of what one actually means: the tooth is not at all misplaced, it does match within a pattern of significance, yet that pattern must not be directly accessible. The incongruous contiguity of tooth with piano key is both crucially relevant, and contrary to all standards of bourgeois good taste: the student's glance of recognition and rejection testifies to the simultaneous presence and repression of the latent signified under the overt layer of meaning. It is in this sense that skilfully handled narrative can speak the manifold truth of signifying forms—this is also, I would suggest, where Galloway shows her artfulness and artistry.

Galloway's stories, therefore, are symbolic centres rather than slices of Scottish life or womanly experience. They speak from the very locus of late twentieth-century experience to those who are no longer seduced by the Victorian Hearts and Flowers. The most fitting metaphor for the creator's choice to reveal the gap under the wallpaper, can again be found nestled in one of the stories:

> It was light and dark at the same time and the walls were moving. They

were sliding and changing colour in huge suppurating spots.... In the middle of the textured ceiling there was a glittering ball of mirror chips, rotating and sparkling light that turned on the wall in formless, spreading blobs. (p. 90)

Thus the modern creator can only take us among the rubble of the fairy tale castle and make us see/hear the stifled suffering and cries. After the shattering of the smoothly reflecting mirror, it is always a consolation to find out that the mirror chips glitter and send out sparkles of light in the night of this world—as the poet Louis Aragon once said, 'Le verre n'est jamais si bleu qu'a sa brisure' ('The glass is at its bluest when it breaks'). It is in this sense that Galloway's writing, like that of her American contemporary William Gass, deserves the term poetic prose.

Works cited

Banfield, Ann (1982) *Unspeakable Sentences*. London: Routledge.

Barthes, Roland (1957) *Mythologies*. Paris: Éditions du Seuil.

Eagleton, Terry (1989) 'Modernism, myth, and monopoly capitalism' in *News from Nowhere*, No 7. Oxford English Limited, pp 19–24.

Galloway, Janice (1991) *Blood*. London: Secker and Warburg.

Lemoine-Luccioni, Eugenie (1971) *Partage des Femmes*. Paris: Points, Seuil.

MacCabe, Colin (1978) *James Joyce and the Revolution of the Word*. London: MacMillan.

McHale, Brian (1987) *Post-Modernist Fiction*. New York: Methuen.

Paccaud-Huguet, Josiane (1991) 'My eppripfftaph: discours nationaliste et parole du sujet dans *Ulysses*' in *Ideologies dans le monde anglo-saxon* No. 4. Université Stendhal, Grenoble, pp. 75–92.

Sibony, Daniel (1982) '*Hamlet* as a writing effect' in *Literature and Psychoanalysis*, ed. S. Felman. Baltimore: The Johns Hopkins University Press.

White, Kenneth (1992) 'Scotland, history and the writer' in *Études écossaises* No. 1. Université Stendhal, Grenoble, GDR Études écossaises, pp. 5–20.

Alienation, 'disappearance strategy' and existentialism

Identity in *The Trick is to Keep Breathing*
and *Foreign Parts*

Darragh O'Grady

Gavin Wallace sees Janice Galloway's work as part of the strong tradition in Scottish literature to write what he terms 'novels of damaged identity'.[1] He claims that 'duality, division and fracture persist as the prevailing creative and critical tools in Scotland' (Wallace 1994, p. 218). This is true of many national literatures but Wallace, importantly, contrasts this Scottish experience with an English one. He explains that, in English novels, 'the deranged, the desperate, the neurotic and the variously addicted might provide the odd deviant diversion to emphasise the reassuring normality of everything else' whereas in Scottish novels 'there are narrators and protagonists, rarely, if ever, fully in control of their existences' (ibid., pp. 217–8). Galloway's protagonists/narrators bear out this analysis. As novelistic characters, they would suggest that it is impossible for 'normal'

---

1. This essay only deals with Janice Galloway's novels but much of what is discussed can be applied to her short story collections: *Blood*, Minerva (1992), and *Where You Find It*, Cape (1996).

identity to be the basis of Scottish narratives because such an identity requires a sense of fixity and Scottish identity is based on a greater degree of fluidity than is assumed to exist in England.

The language of Galloway's texts echoes this fluidity to reinforce her portrayal of an alienated Scottish identity. On one hand, she asserts her texts' Scottishness through the use of Scots. For instance, the use of the word *wean* to mean child (Galloway 1995a, p. 193). Or in *The Trick is to Keep Breathing*: 'It wasny me anyway. Bloody kiwi bloody fruit' (Galloway 1995b, p. 124) The clitic *-ny* in the negative *('wisny')*, here, is cited by Aitken as specific to Scots (Trudgill 1984, p. 104). Besides many striking occurrences of Scots, however, *The Trick is to Keep Breathing* and *Foreign Parts* are written in Scottish English (not to be confused with Standard English spoken in a Scottish accent). The 'overt Scotticisms' (ibid., p. 107) that occur do not mean that her writing is 'in Scots'; they are merely isolated incidents where she uses aspects of the Scots language, possibly for effect or, in a common postcolonial strategy, to mark out her writing as Scottish (as opposed to English). This is interesting when one considers the relative prominence of the West Central Scots of Galloway's native Glasgow in literature and Scottish broadcasting.

An explanation for Galloway's writing in Scottish English might be found in the notion of 'hypercorrection', i.e. the preferred use of prestige forms of language. Hypercorrection has been especially attributed to women where 'in many communities female speakers will use a higher proportion of prestige forms than male speakers' (Coates 1986, p. 67). Jennifer Coates forwards the suggestion that this is due to women's 'insecurity' and 'sensitivity ... to social pressures' (ibid., p. 66). This could be, subconsciously, why Galloway writes in Scottish English rather than the Scots used by male writers such as Irvine Welsh or Hugh MacDiarmid. Scottish English is more prestigious than Scots.

The paradoxical deference towards Englishness on one hand (shown through Galloway's primary use of the prestige form, Scottish English) and nationalistic surety on the other, illustrated by her use of 'overt Scotticisms' (Trudgill 1984, p. 107), reveal a Scottish identity that is unsure of exactly what it is. Such an identity is ambivalent: fluid and fundamentally indefinable, oscillating between feelings of power and powerlessness. Admittedly, every national identity is ambivalent to some degree. As Homi K. Bhabha explains, a national identity that is truly secure in itself does not exist. He points out that beneath 'the comfort of social belonging' there are always the 'hidden injuries of class; ...the powers of political affiliation... the sensibilities of sexuality... [etc.]' (Bhabha 1993, p. 2). However, some nationalities are more alienated than others and the superficial coherence present in, for example, the English culture does not seem to exist in the fractured Scotland that Galloway's books portray.

Bhabha fails to mention a fundamental 'hidden injury' within national identity, i.e. that of gender. Galloway's novels deal with this 'hidden injury'. As with Irvine Welsh's or James Kelman's working-class characters, there is a deep sense in her writing that women have been socially disenfranchised.

Cassie, in *Foreign Parts*, realises this when visiting a museum in France: 'Noble profiles striking grittily determined poses, sinewy limbs etched with striving, turtle plates of muscle on the belly... It was right enough. We weren't in the running at all' (Galloway 1995a, p. 154).

In *The Trick is to Keep Breathing*, Galloway uses dramatic role-play between Joy and various doctors to underline the patriarchal/hierarchical nature of society. This use of role-play points to the arbitrary power relations that structure society, playing on a persistent tradition in dramatic dialogue where one actor adopts a 'high status' role and the other a 'low status' role. (Many actors find it helpful when interacting with each other on stage to think of their character in terms of high or low status, helping them to develop this character and make it more 'real' by contrasting it with another). The fact that this artificial kind of human interaction is happening within a serious context (a hospital where Joy is at her doctors' mercy) underlines the often arbitrary/stilted nature of the power relations between people which structure our society. It can be argued that people often 'perform' in this way, hiding behind roles and a status which they feel helps them to mask any inadequacies or 'hidden injuries'. Of course, like actors, they are really only acting, playing a game. Their status is completely arbitrary within the confines of the many dialogues that form part of their daily lives. Metzstein notes Galloway's use of the dialogue form, describing these parts of the novel as being 'like short scenes from a play script' which take place between Joy and the various men who want her to play the game of 'pliant other' (Metzstein 1993, pp. 140–1).

Joy Stone's obsessive ritualisation is another way in which Galloway reveals *internalised* social control techniques that are, effectively, a form of self-policing: '*The Bathing Ritual...* The cold water runs on while I sit and soap each leg in turn, then lift the razor, checking the edge is keen. It gives a better finish slicing upward against the hair: it severs more closely. I have to be careful it doesn't catch or draw blood. That would be unsightly... I put on my prettiest underwear: net lace and satin, ribbon straps…' (ibid., p.47) All this effort is a deference towards society's expectations of an 'attractive' woman's appearance. As with an alienated Scottish identity that concurrently rejects and accepts Englishness, Joy is privately defiant in the face of Dr. Stead but still accepts the value judgements of a society that allots power to the doctor and powerlessness to the patient.

This gender issue exists alongside the specific 'injury' of being Scottish within the United Kingdom. Therefore, being a Scottish woman produces an even deeper sense of ambivalent identity than, for example, being an English or French woman. Furthermore, Galloway's characters are, to a degree, socially disenfranchised because of their class. Alienation exists, therefore, on three levels: class, national marginalisation and, perhaps most importantly, through her protagonists' position within patriarchy. As the Scottish poet Jackie Kay states: '…the point about her characters is that they don't feel at home in Scotland.'[2]

The escape from the subjective complexities of Scottish identity is a major theme in Galloway's work. She treats of the postmodern escapes of tourism, shopping, drug use and media-consumption. These postmodern escapes are usefully explained by Baudrillard's theory of 'disappearance strategy'. He argues that the subject, through engaging in these various activities, 'disappears' into a superficial, objective existence where the complexities of subjective identity can be escaped; temporarily, at least.

Tourism allows the individual to escape the subjective environment of 'home', and experience the objective landscape of 'foreign parts' or the 'unheimlich', to use the Freudian term. In these objective surroundings, the traveller sheds national identity, unrooted in the foreign social structure. When touring, Cassie and Rona temporarily shed their Scottish identity by travelling in an unfamiliar environment, taking on the identity of the surroundings and thereby experiencing hyperreal objectivity. For Baudrillard, this shedding of subjective identity and escape into objectivity is a form of 'disappearance'. The indigenous culture is commodified by the tourist who consumes a landscape of museums, cathedrals, churches, restaurants. The individual, through his/her consumption of these universal cultural signifiers, loses all subjectivity and becomes objective, moving behind the screen of 'networks and models': 'What are they; what do they do; what do they become behind this screen? They turn themselves into an impenetrable and

---

2. *In Your Face: Janice Galloway,* 4/12/1995, BBC 2, 11.15pm.

meaningless surface, which is a method of disappearing. They eclipse themselves; they melt into the superficial screen in such a way that their reality... may be radically questioned' (Baudrillard 1988, pp.213–4). In other words, by touring, tourists 'disappear' into hyperreality, becoming hyperreal themselves.

This hyperreal 'disappearance' is attractive to the individual because he/she, through entry into superficial or 'aleatory' (ibid, p.149) objectivity, loses all sense of subjectivity/specificity together with all its unresolved/unresolvable complexities. In this way, the acute alienation of Scottish identity discussed above can be escaped.

The complexities of history and culture are hyperreal for the tourist, reduced to simplistic, superficial representations that reject interpretation. The rejection of interpretation is attractive and, therefore, memorable: 'Cassie tried to think what she knew about Eleanor of Aquitaine... All she could come up with was Katharine Hepburn looking broken-hearted and defiant in a film... Films did that. They contained your imagination, packaged even real things up in wee parcels you couldn't get rid of... the bones of three of the most powerful political forces in Medieval Europe were inside these stone shells at Cassie's feet... And Cassie knew damn all about them. *Not anything real*' (Galloway 1995a, p.165) [my emphasis]. Cassie's touristic knowledge here is 'not anything real' because it is hyperreal. She realises that watching a film is a hyperreal experience, it 'contains your imagination'. The subject 'disappears' into the screen of floating signifiers (the film-screen), drawn into a hyperreality where interpretation is unnecessary and the simulacra are 'packaged... up in wee parcels', ready for consumption.

Bryan Turner notes that the car screen and the TV screen have a number of things in common: 'The passenger, like the viewer, is passive, indifferent, entertained and perhaps over-stimulated by the flashing trivia of the landscape and the scene' (Turner 1993, p.153). In this way, watching a television or film-screen is like the experience of driving/tourist cruising. Like film/TV viewing, reading an environment 'through the car screen is a voyeuristic consumption of a series of signs... [a] detached and therefore cynical cruise through hyperreality' (ibid., p.154).

Cassie notices this about Rona's driving. Rona becomes detached, 'disappearing' into hyperreality, concentrating on the road ahead with the same attention she would give to her television screen: 'Rona didn't often chat when she was driving... She could drive for miles sometimes and *not even seem to be awake,* the way she drove to the office in the mornings and said O we're here when she was turning into the car park like it was a surprise. But it couldn't be the case, not really... the thought that large numbers of people, unbeknown to non-drivers, were careering about on the road, *not even conscious* maybe, avoiding death by sheer luck. It wasn't possible. Cassie sneaked a look at Rona to check...' (Galloway 1995a, p. 20) [my emphasis]. Rona's surprise at turning into the office car park ('O we're here...') echoes Baudrillard's statement in *America*: 'Driving is a spectacular form of amnesia. Everything to be discovered, everything to be obliterated' (Baudrillard, 1989: 9). Her hypnotic, hyperreal state ends when she encounters the familiar, her place of work. Baudrillard describes this running 'up against a familiar landscape, or some decipherable message' as a breaking of the 'spell' (ibid: 9-10): '...the amnesic, ascetic, asymptomatic charm of disappearance succumbs to affect and worldly semiology' (ibid., p. 10).

Galloway herself admits fascination with cruising in her car: 'I like driving through the city at night... Looping in and out of motorways near cities, driving round about cities because... there are lights, there are signs. I guess it's all to do with the fact that it looks so *easy*: you've got your narrative, you've got your linear line. If you just follow that line you go some place and you do it and it's true. It's like an affirmation that life is, in fact, easy. You follow the arrows and you get where they say you're going to go.' [Galloway's emphasis]

The driving experience for Rona becomes even more hyperreal in France because *everything* is unfamiliar. More concentration is required. There is no familiar, 'worldly semiology' to break the 'spell' of 'disappearance': '...Rona's hands were gripping the wheel, knuckles white. It was because she was driving. She would be concentrating on the other side of the road thing, that would be it.' (Galloway 1995a, p. 20). This experience of the unfamiliar reinforces the initial reason for tourism as a means to achieving the ultimate in hyperreal 'disappearance'. Rona and Cassie are, effectively, 'cruising' through France. It is important that Galloway has given them no fixed itinerary. The only fixities in their holiday are the starting and finishing dates. This drifting rootlessness has been noted by Kate Chisholm in *The Sunday Telegraph,* where she notes that *Foreign Parts* is 'a road movie for feminists...'

Turner compares 'cruising' to 'channel-hopping', the viewing practice of hopping between different TV channels at regular intervals as interest wanes: 'The couch potato, in experiencing everything visually, is involved in nothing in practice. The experience of car-cruising by strangers or tourists sampling a landscape is very similar' (Turner 1993, p. 154). Timothy Corrigan, in his discussion of road movies, agrees: 'As with the movie experience, time on the road becomes figurative space' (Corrigan 1991, p.146). The cruiser consumes the '...(hysterical) excess of indeterminable possibilities' (ibid., p.147) as he/she hurtles through empty space. Rona and Cassie are the ultimate cruisers, 'fraudulent moochers in other people's territory, getting by on the cheap' (Galloway 1995a, p.150).

One of the most popular methods of escape from Scottish identity within Scotland itself would seem to be drug use. Taking drugs is a form of 'disappearance strategy'. As with tourism, drug-taking is an attempt to escape the specificity and complexities of subjectivity in search of an 'aleatory' (Baudrillard 1988, p.149), i.e. superficial, objectivity. Drug use is central to modern identity as a form of self-escape. As is borne out in Edinburgh's infamous heroin problem during the 1980s, it seems especially prevalent in Scotland where it is used as a 'disappearance strategy' to avoid the acute alienation discussed above. Wallace notes this self-anaesthetisation in his discussion of the Scottish novel as 'novel of damaged identity'. He describes Scotland as 'a country with a permanent spiritual hangover'. (Wallace 1994, p.226) Irvine Welsh deals with this in *Trainspotting* where Tommy paraphrases Gavin Wallace's point in less academic terms: 'Iggy Pop looks right at us as he sings the line: "America takes drugs in psychic defence"; only he changes "America" for "Scatlin", and defines us mair accurately in a single sentence than all the others have ever done...' (Welsh 1993, p.75).

Joy Stone, in *The Trick is to Keep Breathing*, also uses drugs (alcohol with anti-depressants) as a means of escape from subjective identity. As Galloway says, she's anaesthetising herself:[3]

> Gin tastes sweet and bitter at the same time, stripping down in clean lines, blooming like an acid flower in the pit of my stomach... If I get drunk enough I won't have to go to work tomorrow... This is cheering and helps me through another mouthful. (Galloway 1995b, p.88).

Taking alcohol and anti-depressants is not the only method of disappearance that Joy uses, however. She consumes large amounts of media as a form of escapism. She is hypnotically drawn to the theatrical display of simulacra that the media holds:

---

3. Telephone conversation with Janice Galloway, 27/6/1996

...Tonight I know what to do. I have a new magazine.

> Jupiter in your sign makes you resilient... Just remember when
> the going gets tough, the tough get going! Big changes are on
> their way, if you are patient enough to let them develop.

Baked Alaska—new style.
Making the most of Summer's late harvest.
Our Best Ever Chocolate Cake.
7 Meals that make in Minutes.
Diet for a firmer new you!

Converting a Victorian schoolhouse into a des res!
(Galloway 1995b, p. 27)

The irony of an anorexic with little or no money reading recipes and an article on how to convert a Victorian schoolhouse into a des res is all too obvious. The horoscope's promise that 'big changes are on their way' is also ironic if the reader bears Joy's grim situation in mind. This irony underlines the meaninglessness of both Joy's media consumption and the information the media contains. These magazine captions are 'ritualistic' *à la* Baudrillard (1988, p. 149) in that they are all consumable clichés, repeated over and over again in countless magazines and even in countless issues of the same magazine. Joy is attracted to this very meaninglessness and repetition. The media rejects interpretation. As for the Ecstasy dancer, it is the 'aleatory, meaningless or ritualistic and meticulous, circulation of signs on the surface' (ibid., p. 149) that draws Joy.

For Joy, media-consumption as 'disappearance strategy' spills over into consumption of goods through shopping. Like all consumers, she finds the supermarket a site of hyperreal disappearance: 'TESCO's. Red neon all the way to the other end of the precincts, pointing the way to lights, rows of pretty boxes, pastels and primaries, tinsel colours; tins, sealed packets begging to be burst. I get dry and warm just thinking about the supermarket. It makes me feel rich and I don't need to think. I can spend hours among the buckle-wheeled trolleys... numbing my fingers on the bags of frozen broccoli... I go to the drinks aisle and read the labels over and over, teasing myself with which one I'll buy (Galloway 1995b, p. 24). The supermarket is a place where Joy can shed her subjective identity and enter into the objective world of simulacra. This particular hyperreal 'disappearance' of the consumer recurs in *Foreign Parts*. Cassie loses herself in the hyperreal world of the 'hypermarket', most easily accessible by car (another central feature of the consumer society) (Galloway 1995a, p.118).

Galloway herself acknowledges a fascination with the shopping area and its effect on women: '…I come here for hours, watching women in a state of semi-vulnerability, where they're concentrating on something. What do they think they're buying? …I'm never quite sure what *I'm* doing… they reveal things that maybe they wouldn't articulate.'[4] [Galloway's emphasis] Dean and Juliet MacCannell usefully summarise Baudrillard's definition of consumerism as a 'collective hysteria that takes the form of manic appropriation of an endless series of objects' (Porter 1993, p.127). This 'manic appropriation' is not a search for meaning, however, but rather, as with media consumption, a search for that which Joy terms as 'soothing' (Galloway 1995b, p.37), the search for the hypnotic state where the individual can lose his/her identity in a hyperreality where privilege has moved from the subject to the object.

Shoppers, tourists, drug users: all are defined as such by their respective 'disappearances' into hyperreality. For Porter, in his article 'Baudrillard: history, hysteria and consumption', drug use and consumerism are inextricably linked as effects of capitalism, whether it is at the end of the twentieth century or the end of the eighteenth century. Consumption is, therefore, an umbrella term under which we can put tourism, drug-use, media-consumption and shopping. All these activities involve the consumption of meaningless signifiers in the search for a hypnotic 'disappearance' into hyperreality where the complexities of subjective identity can be escaped.

This escape is only temporary, however. In Galloway's novels, the escape into hyperreal objectivity is balanced with a consistent return to subjective identity. Baudrillard's general philosophy of simulation and pervasive hyperreality, while its aspect of 'disappearance strategy' is a useful means of discussing post-modern escapism, cannot be applied as a whole to Galloway's novels. For Baudrillard, history has reached the 'Third Order of Simulacra' where the distinctions of fiction and the real have been abolished by an all-pervasive hyperreality in which all signifiers have become self-referential. In other words, the consumer experiences discussed above are not temporary

---

4.   *In Your Face: Janice Galloway*, 4/12/1995, BBC 2, 11.15pm.

escape strategies at all but rather, are currently our complete experience of life. In this hyperreality, therefore, objectivity has become prioritised over subjectivity.

There are three central problems with all of this. Firstly, hyperreality is not endless in *The Trick is to Keep Breathing* and *Foreign Parts*. 'Disappearance strategy' is only a temporary escape from a subjective reality to which Galloway's protagonists always return. There is a return to the real from the hyperreal. Her characters never permanently remain in the supermarket/on holiday/drugged. Secondly, Baudrillard's supposed deprioritisation of subjectivity implies the impossibility of specificity. As is detailed above, these novels are extremely specific vis-à-vis language and nationality. The third problem with applying Baudrillard's theories as a whole to Galloway's writing is that subjectivity has not been deprioritised by objectivity in her novels. Rather, subjectivity is a central theme.

Gavin Wallace notes in Galloway's work a 'forensic fascination with the problematics of identity' (Wallace 1994, p.225). Her novel proposes that subjectivity, psychology and, indeed, the 'subconscious' (a term that Baudrillard sees as a Freudian construct rendered invalid in today's aleatory superficial society) are not yet dead. Galloway claims to write 'from as subconscious a basis as possible', her first novel concerning a psychologically and socially alienated protagonist. Alienation is impossible in hyperreality: all signifiers become self-referential and there is no self/other dichotomy. This is why 'disappearance strategy' is so attractive for the alienated.

On the other hand, Galloway's novels do not prioritise the subjective over the objective. Rather, there is a constant interplay between subjectivity and objectivity; a paradoxical co-existence of subjective identity and objective hyperreality that both underlines the post-modern aspects of these novels and echoes the fundamental ambivalence of Scottish identity. *The Trick is to Keep Breathing* and *Foreign Parts* both illustrate an oscillation between subjective and objective within their protagonists, ending with the return to a subjectivity that always seems just about to collapse back into objectivity.

Therefore, Galloway's assertion of subjectivity is within a continual oscillation between the subjective and the objective that is uncontained by the traditional denouement of the novel. Near the end of *The Trick is to Keep Breathing*, Joy Stone asserts a new self, accepting her lover's drowning in an existential move. As Wallace points out, she finally finds an assertive subjective voice: 'I hear it quite distinctly, my own voice inside the empty house. I forgive you' (Galloway 1995b, p.235). She also makes several other assertions of her subjectivity: 'I want to be ready for the surprises … I have to learn to submit to terrifying chaos and not revert… I have to stop reading these fucking magazines' (ibid., p.223). Not 'reverting' and stopping 'reading… magazines' is a rejection of 'disappearance strategy'. While this seems, on one hand, to be an affirmative ending to the novel for Joy's subjectivity, Galloway's strong belief that one should examine 'the light with the dark' shines through. *The Trick is to Keep Breathing* escapes a neat closure that would privilege either subjectivity or objectivity. The reader feels that Joy's self-anaesthetisation will continue. The ending of the novel is the beginning of yet another alcoholic stupor: 'Just now I have the whiskey… The tree lights. Wee *diversions…*' (ibid., p.234 [my emphasis]. Furthermore, the assertive actions of selling her dry-rotting cottage and learning to swim (her mother *and* her lover died of drowning) are both only *contemplated:* 'Maybe I could learn to swim…' (ibid., p.235).

The close of Galloway's *Foreign Parts* deals with the same necessity for the acceptance of the oscillation between objectivity and subjectivity. There is a more cheerful acceptance of fluidity here than in *The Trick is to Keep Breathing*: 'I know we'll manage. Me and Rona. We'll be absolutely fine… Sober this time' (Galloway 1995a, p.262). Interestingly, sobriety is affirmed at the end of this novel (whereas *The Trick is to Keep Breathing* ends with a drunken Joy). However, as with the possible continuation of Joy's alcohol habit, the reader must ask: 'do I believe that Rona and Cassie will really be "sober this time"?' The continued 'disappearance strategy' of drinking alcohol is a distinct possibility. Galloway's characters' continued escape in hyperreality does not, however, imply an 'inauthentic existence'. They are aware of their subjectivity and balance this awareness with an escape into objectivity (this is further discussed below). Therefore, subjectivity and objectivity co-exist in her novels. Her characters, in existentialist terms, ultimately embrace 'authentic existence'.

Galloway follows more established writers like James Kelman in the Scottish literary tradition of existentialism. While it would be problematic to declare Scottish novels more 'existential' than English novels, there is a link between existentialist and Scottish literatures that critics and writers alike have noted. Janice Galloway, for example, sees herself as having more in common with French, Russian and East European existentialists (such as Sartre, Dostoyevsky and Kafka) than with English novelists. This could be an attempt to assert an independence from British culture through alignment with international literatures (a common post-colonial strategy) but many feel that the comparison is valid. Cairns Craig describes Kelman's characters as coming at Being 'by negating the systems of thought through which we enclose and tame existence' (Craig 1993, p.111). Galloway's characters do exactly the same. They consistently attack the arbitrary structures and falsities that form our society, that 'tame existence'.

Galloway proposes that society is arbitrarily constructed. Whereas Welsh and Kelman approach the issue from the point of view of class and nationality, she deals primarily with the arbitrariness of gender roles. She labels these arbitrary structures social 'myths' or 'lies': 'Our lives have been mythologised and codified by modern power groups whoever they may be… there are layers and layers of lies, of '*mauvaise foi*' to use an existential phrase, or quite simply silences… about what female experience is.'[5]

The notion that society is a large construct of lies runs through all of Galloway's work. Joy constantly questions society's adherence to this construct in *The Trick is to Keep Breathing*:

> Other people. Other people interest me. How they manage. There are several possibilities.
>
> 1. They are just as confused as me but they aren't letting on.
> 2. They don't know what the point is.
> 3. They don't understand they don't know what the point is.
> 4. They don't mind they don't know what the point is.
> 5. They don't even know there are any questions.
> (Galloway 1995b, p.198)

The importance of questioning and the rejection of an 'inauthentic' existence where there is a complete unawareness of the self and its subjective/objective aspects are both crucial for Galloway. In *Foreign Parts* she humorously deconstructs the futile exercise of tourism, which she sees society as blindly accepting in an act of consumption. As Baudrillard suggests in his earlier work, current consumption is not undertaken out of any intrinsic need but, rather, because there is a capitalistic control of meaning that urges the individual to consume large quantities of meaningless signifiers in order to feel his/her existence as, in some way, justified: '…Folk sitting on the shale hungry for sea and getting rain, half-stripped among the limpets and

---

5. Ibid.

mouldering, limbless starfish, *determinedly going about the summer.*' (Galloway 1995a, pp.219–20) [emphasis added].

Baudrillard also theorises that we holiday in order to experience 'super-banality', a form of hyperreality:

> …a human being can find a much deeper boredom while on vacation than in daily life… How can one imagine that people would repudiate their everyday life in search of an alternative? On the contrary, they make it their destiny: by intensifying it in the appearances of the contrary; by submerging themselves to the point of ecstasy; and by fixating monotony in an even greater one. (Baudrillard 1988, p.200)

Galloway captures this futile embrace of monotony in *Foreign Parts*: 'This is the life, says Rona… Nothing else happens for five minutes, then Rona pours us both some more cider… Ah, she says. The Life. Another five minutes. Eventually Cassie says… Rona?' (Galloway 1995a, p.243). Cassie and Rona's tourism is essentially futile but they tour because it gives their lives some sort of definition.

Photography is an essential part of holiday making: 'Cassie took a picture… Smile. You're on holidays … Christ' (ibid., p.118). It is evidence that the holiday has actually occurred, reinforcing the tourist's super-banal identity as 'tourist':

> Rona took lots of pictures … It was one of the things Rona did … You were supposed to smile in photos as proof a) that you really had been there and b) it wasn't awful all the time. It was evidence. In case. Cassie couldn't think what the case might be but the photos were proof against it anyway. (ibid., pp.202–3)

Photography also maintains the social construct of lies/myths that Galloway so vehemently attacks. It documents a particular version of history and identity. It is also a method by which the individual can capture a (false) feeling of fixity in an unfixed and often self-referential world. The ludicrousness of this futile photography is a reflection of the larger arbitrary construct that Galloway is attempting to topple.

Through all these novels' existential impulse, subjectivity is addressed and an authentic existence affirmed. An authentic existence is one that is acutely aware of the necessary oscillation between the subjective and objective within identity. The constant temporary escape from subjectivity is quite conscious for Galloway's protagonists, a sort of purposeful self-anaesthetisation. This is a form of self-assertion in itself through its existential awareness of subjectivity's relationship to objectivity. Joy ultimately recognises, in an existential move, that even though existence is fundamentally meaningless, we must continue to exist without despair in the face of this meaninglessness, recognising the strategies with which we arbitrarily construct reassuring meaning. This echoes Beckett's protagonist's existential statement in 'The Unnameable': '…you must go on, I can't go on, I'll go on' (Beckett 1979, p. 382). Joy's multi-faceted 'disappearance strategy' embraces the aleatory and the meaningless but she welcomes this objectivity with a clear sense of her own subjectivity. There is a concurrent assertion of/escape from selfhood:

> I have to take the pills because they will make me accept … Maybe they will make me stop wanting to know the answer. Maybe the pills know the answer. I doubt it but I have no proof … I stand on the slope of the hill and look down at the street that is not a film. This is the Way Things Are Now. I touch the wood round the door, the crust of the brick. My knuckles scrape the brick and the skin peels. I look at the blood and try to believe I'm here, that the wood and brick are the truth. The knowledge of this fact. There is no dream and no waking up. This is today. (Galloway 1995b, pp. 96–7)

Here, drunkenly, Joy sees a fusion of the 'real' and the hyperreal. The constant oscillation between objectivity and subjectivity has blurred into one state: 'There is no dream and no waking up.' She must existentially accept this 'real'/hyperreal fusion: 'This is the Way Things Are Now… This is today.'

One thing is certain in these novels and that is the acceptance of the paradox of play between subjective and objective, illustrated in the last paragraph of *Foreign Parts* where Cassie describes a stone that does not sink in water because it is skidding along the surface: 'That the skin of the water should be tough enough is a constant surprise'. (Galloway 1995a, p. 262). The subject (stone) skims along the surface of superficial objectivity (skin of the water). It is only when this play between subject and objectivity ceases that the stone sinks. The lack of closure in Galloway's novels allows for an infinite interplay between subjective and objective. She promotes the necessity of accepting the ambivalence of identity and regarding lack of closure with optimism. Gavin Wallace would agree, seeing contemporary 'Scottish literary imagination' as 'exploring newly-enabling, exciting and more affirmative directions' (Wallace 1994, p.225). Rather than simply depicting 'damaged identity', Janice Galloway's novels are examining the various possible resolutions to such an identity. They both point in one direction, however: that the trick is to keep living.

Works cited

Aitken, A.J. (1984) 'Scottish Accents and Dialects', in *Language in the British Isles*, edited by Peter Trudgill. Cambridge: Cambridge University Press.

Anderson, Carol (1994) 'Listening to the Women Talk', in *The Scottish Novel Since the Seventies*, edited by Gavin Wallace and Randall Stevenson. Edinburgh: Edinburgh University Press [1993].

Baudrillard, Jean (1989) *America*, translated by Chris Turner, London: Verso [1988].

Baudrillard, Jean (1988) *Selected Writings: Jean Baudrillard*. edited by Mark Poster, Cambridge: Polity Press.

Beckett, Samuel (1979) *The Trilogy*, London: Picador [1959].

Beveridge, Craig and Turnbull, Ronald (1989) *The Eclipse of Scottish Culture*. Edinburgh: Polygon.

Bhabha, Homi K. (1990) 'Introduction', in *Nation and Narration*, edited by Homi K. Bhabha. London: Routledge.

Coates, Jennifer (1993) *Women, Men and Language*, London: Longman Studies in Language and Linguistics [1986].

Corrigan, Timothy (1991) *A Cinema Without Walls*. London: Routledge.

Craig, Cairns (1994) 'Resisting Arrest: James Kelman', in *The Scottish Novel Since the Seventies*, edited by Gavin Wallace and Randall Stevenson. Edinburgh: Edinburgh University Press [1993].

Galloway, Janice (1992) *Blood*. London: Minerva [1991].

—— (1995a) *Foreign Parts*. London: Vintage [1992].

—— (1995b) *The Trick is to Keep Breathing*. London: Minerva [1989].

—— (1996) *Where You Find It*. London: Cape.

McClure, J. Derrick (1979) 'Scots: its Range of Uses.', in *Languages of Scotland*, edited by A.J. Aitken and T. McArthur. London: Chambers.

Melechi, Antonio (1993) 'The Ecstasy of Disappearance', in *Popular Cultural Studies 1: Rave Off. Politics and Deviance in Contemporary Youth Culture*. 3d. Steve Redhead, Avebury, Aldershot.

Metzstein, Margery (1994) 'Of Myths and Men: Aspects of Gender in the Fiction of Janice Galloway.', in *The Scottish Novel Since the Seventies*, edited by Gavin Wallace and Randall Stevenson. Edinburgh: Edinburgh University Press.

Morgan, Edwin (1994) 'Tradition and Experiment in the Glasgow Novel', in *The Scottish Novel Since the Seventies*, edited by Gavin Wallace and Randall Stevenson. Edinburgh: Edinburgh University Press [1993].

Porter, Roy (1993) 'Baudrillard: history, hysteria and consumption', in *Forget Baudrillard?*, edited by Chris Rojek and Bryan S. Turner. London: Routledge.

Turner, Bryan (1993) 'Cruising America', in *Forget Baudrillard?*, edited by Chris Rojek and Bryan S. Turner. London: Routledge.

Wallace, Gavin (1994) 'Voices in Empty Houses: The Novel of Damaged Identity', in *The Scottish Novel Since the Seventies*, edited by Gavin Wallace and Randall Stevenson. Edinburgh: Edinburgh University Press [1993].

Welsh, Irvine (1996) *Trainspotting*. London: Minerva [1993].

The silencing of the little lambs

Expression and repression in *Clara*

Ailsa Crum

> If language were liquid
> It would be rushing in
> Instead here we are
> In a silence more eloquent
> Than any word could ever be...[1]

Suzanne Vega's hushed and haunting voice seeps towards me from the direction of the radio as I watch myself, reading, in the corner of the room. It's an appropriate accompaniment for Janice Galloway's latest novel, *Clara*.[2] Galloway has said that the 'most interesting aspect... to write about... became the unsaids, the silences raddling the life'.[3] The life in question is that of Clara Wieck Schumann, the young girl with the overbearing father who became one of the most renowned concert pianists of her time, who married Robert Schumann and... lived so that Janice Galloway could tell the tale.

The publisher's notes inside the front cover begin by stating that this novel is a 'radical departure' from Galloway's previous work, although they do go on

---

1. Suzanne Vega, 'Language', *Solitude Standing*. A&M Records, 1986.
2. Janice Galloway, *Clara*. London: Jonathan Cape, 2002.
3. Janice Galloway, 'Silent Partner'. *The Guardian*, 20 June 2002.

to indicate that it is 'primarily about timeless, common things'. Other than the fact that the central character of the novel is a historical figure (or, more accurately, the wife of a historical figure—of which, more later), I would dispute that this novel is a departure for Galloway at all. It is about the timeless, common things that Galloway has been writing about for years. If Clara Schumann hadn't actually existed, Galloway would undoubtedly have made her up. By writing about her in this way there is, of course, a sense in which she has done exactly that.

Mary McGlynn has identified what she considers are the 'major concerns' of Galloway's fiction: 'women's secondary status in society, the complexities of inhabiting a body… the purposes and possibilities of formal experiment, the functions and effects of social class structures, and the intricacies of family dynamics.'[4] All of which can readily be identified in *Clara* and some of which I'll return to later in this piece.

In an article on 'writing and not writing' her second novel, *Foreign Parts*, Galloway states 'It's hardly contentious to say that a significant number of Scottish novels are more notable for their preoccupation [with] what is *not* said rather than what *is;* with the struggle to find a "voice"'.[5] Here, Galloway could have been describing any of her work, and certainly the notion of finding a voice is a central theme in *Clara*.

The story of Clara Wieck Schumann is intriguing in itself, but the novel is something else, something more. Its geometry is fascinating. Just as in geometry—where the lines are of less importance, less significance, perhaps, than the spaces between them and the shapes that they contain—so the words in the novel are only one part of the whole. It's the untold parts of this tale that have real resonance.

The novel is structured around one of Robert Schumann's song cycles, 'Woman's Life and Love'—an interesting choice given that Clara also composed. But this book isn't about the life of Clara Schumann. It's about the life of Clara Schumann under the control of two men: first her father and later her husband. That the structure of the story should be dictated by one of those men is, like everything in Galloway's fiction, of great significance. The geometry doesn't end there. There are circles, parallels, and points of tangency within and beyond the book itself—and, of course, there are the ellipses.

---

4.   Mary McGlynn, Profile of Janice Galloway, *Review of Contemporary Fiction* Summer 2001. Illinois State University.

5.   Janice Galloway, 'Tongue in my Ear: on writing and not writing Foreign Parts', *Review of Contemporary Fiction*. Dalkey Archive Press, Chicago, 1995.

Clara doesn't talk much, she was four years old before she uttered a sound and that diffidence extends into adulthood. As a child she witnesses her domineering father control the steady line of boys, girls, men, women who come to him for music lessons.

Sing!
Someone does. She has never heard anyone refuse. The very idea.
Sing! (p. 15)

'*The voice is your beginning!*' her father shouts. 'It's how every lesson starts' (p. 16). It's how it starts for Clara; how she finally chooses to express herself. Middle C is the first sound she utters of all the notes on a vast keyboard: 'C for Clara' (p. 20). Clara's mother is a singer and concert pianist, but she 'has the house to run' (p. 17) and anyway Clara's father had determined, before she was ever born, that she should be 'the greatest pianist he could fashion, his brightness, a star'. (p. 23)

Clara's father is also determined that this great life should be recorded and so he begins her diary, which he writes on her behalf and in the first person. So one of his entries reads '*Father deserves my greatest devotion and gratitude for his ceaseless efforts on my behalf*' (p. 61). The entries he doesn't write personally, he dictates or edits after she has drafted them. This represents one of many cyclical circumstances within the novel; there is a clear link between these early beginnings and her later life married to Robert Schumann. It is Robert's idea that they should begin a marriage diary—his is the first entry on the day of their wedding. He declares that they should share everything that affects their household and marriage in its pages. And yet he is not above correcting and editing Clara's entries. But this repression of Clara's opportunities to express herself is not the final word.

Clara's father may have fantasised that he fashioned her as a great pianist, but it is she who becomes the 'virtuosa'. Many people clamour to hear what it was about his teaching that generated her success—the failure to identify any set of actions on his behalf that was different from his training of countless others, hints that the special talent was hers. Similarly, a hand injury effectively ends any hopes Robert Schumann had been harbouring of following the young Clara onto the stage as a concert pianist. So, while the regime he instates in their marital home makes it difficult for Clara to practise—when he is not using the single piano himself for composing, he demands that the house be kept in silence—it is she, not he, who can play his compositions before the public. It is she, then, who brings his work to life, who expresses it before the audiences who come to hear *her* play. His name alone not yet a major attraction—on tour he receives gifts sent to their hotel addressed to '*Clara Schumann's husband*' (p. 264).

Beyond the novel itself, a further angle in the geometry of the tale is the obvious fact that, by writing this work, Galloway is speaking on behalf of Clara and, although she has chosen to write in the third person, she is nonetheless performing a further edit on Clara's life, directing a new diary. And then, there are Clara's own compositions. Though few in number by direct comparison with her husband's, she has left this legacy. A similarity between the lives of Clara and Galloway could be identified in relation to both women's creative work. Galloway has recorded how her own sister dogmatically and violently told her 'women canny write',[6] literally hitting the young Janice if she mistakenly took books by female authors home from the library. There are softer echoes of this in *Clara*. It is indicated that, while it may be acceptable for a woman to become a celebrated pianist, actually composing the music to be played really is man's work. Even Robert Schumann, who sometimes encourages her composition as an activity she can undertake without leaving home, also corrects her harmony, editing her work. In a separate piece, Galloway has highlighted the most frequently found quote from Clara Schumann in which she dismisses her *Trio*, Op. 7 as 'women's work, which lacks force and occasionally, invention'. Although Galloway also quotes Brahms as having written: 'By rights, I should have to inscribe all my best melodies "really by Clara Schumann". I have you to thank for more melodies than all the passages of such things you take from me.' In her own words, Galloway continues: 'we assume [Brahms] is merely being charming… when it comes to Clara's remark, we assume she is merely being accurate'.[7]

We could hide from this fact and tell ourselves that there has been a world of social progress since the nineteenth century, what with the advent of feminism, post-feminism even. And yet, despite the awards, the critical acclaim and wide readership Galloway's work has attracted, in August 2002 I attended a book launch at the Glasgow branch of Borders at which I heard a celebrated professor of Scottish Literature describe Galloway's work in passing as

---

6.   Janice Galloway, 'Objective Truth and the Grinding Machine (how I started writing)', for Edinburgh International Book Festival publication, republished in *A Scottish Childhood*, 1998.

7.   Janice Galloway, 'Why do they shut me out of Heaven? Do I sing too loud?', text of a staged event commissioned for Mayfest 1995.

'women's writing'. Earlier in the same sentence he reeled off the names of other contemporary Scottish writers—James Kelman, Alasdair Gray, Irvine Welsh—without apparently feeling the need to describe their work as 'men's writing'.

While the treatment of gender within *Clara* may be one of the most immediate features of the novel, there is coverage too of that other Galloway hallmark, silencing on the grounds of social class. The treatment of this in *Clara* emphasises another point of tangency between the lives of Janice Galloway and Clara Schumann. It was at university, Galloway indicates in an interview with Donny O'Rourke, that she became interested in how she spoke: 'what that meant and implied', she continues, 'there was a personal subtext a lot of the time that said how working class people spoke was wrong.'[8] In *Clara* the 'aristocrats and their support machine, officialdom' comment on Clara Schumann's 'lumpy Saxon accent… an accent, moreover, she made no attempt to hide'. (p. 266) The observation in the novel becomes more explicit, extending to Robert and including all artists:

> Artists *themselves* might come kissed with greatness of a kind, but few were well-bred and Madame Schumann, as if wearing a torn petticoat, let it show. She moved prettily among the malachite tables and gilded palms, she understood which fork was which, but when she opened her mouth—alas! There was the teacher's daughter they knew her to be. Her husband was a bookbinder's boy and almost entirely self-taught. As hired entertainment went, however, Madame Schumann was superior. (p. 267)

This represents her social isolation or exclusion from the audiences who, on the face of it, come to hear her. It also points to the fact that, while having the freedom to express herself is important, the values the listeners place on her 'voice' is the other side of the equation. There are similarities with *The Trick is to Keep Breathing*. The main character there, Joy Stone, is a teacher who, as the lover of a married colleague, is unable to fit in at school. Later she is excluded from 'society' within the mental hospital that she finally agrees to attend—both by the staff, who continually expect her to conform to their stereotypical notion of a teacher, and by the other patients, who believe she considers herself to be better than them.[9] It is interesting that Clara doesn't

---

8. Donny O'Rourke, 'The Conversation: reflections of returning writers', *Avenue* No. 21. University of Glasgow, January 1997.
9. Janice Galloway, *The Trick is to Keep Breathing*. Edinburgh: Polygon, 1989.

attempt to conceal her 'lumpy Saxon accent'. No doubt this is intended to confirm her status as an outsider, but it could also be interpreted as representing Clara's strength of character that she refuses to use a voice other than her own.

But it wasn't the public performances and the necessary round of post-concert pressing of aristocratic flesh that most interested Galloway in Clara Schumann. Galloway has written: 'Clara, then, the good domestic woman, was what thrilled me. Her silences and her piano-playing were survival tools—she made her utterances between them. The device of fiction is what permits silence to speak, to find the edges of a psychology and bring it not only into being, but entirely close to home.' (p.3)

Despite the similarity between the central themes of *Clara* and those of Galloway's other work, Clara Schumann is an unusual choice of central character for Galloway. This is because of Clara's strength, her ability to get by. The recurrent refrain of those around her saying, verbally or non-verbally, 'you'll do', is reminiscent of Joy Stone in *The Trick is to Keep Breathing* repeatedly asking variations on the theme of 'What will I do while I'm getting by?', the difference being that it is others who bestow the compliment—albeit a rather limited one—on Clara. Unlike Joy Stone, Clara Schumann was not dependent on the two men in her life, her demonic father and demented husband. Despite being brought up by her father in the most oppressive of circumstances, including being forced to witness first hand her father's brutal physical abuse of her brothers, Clara still had the courage and inner resolve to disobey his express wishes by marrying Robert Schumann. Her silence and piano playing were certainly trusty survival tools in her father's household. But, while she had high hopes of her marriage to Robert heralding a time of boundless 'permissions', she had to endure the vagaries of his behaviour as he struggled with devastating mental illness. In this instance she clung to that womanly survival tool—domesticity—to keep her going, to make sure she'd continue to 'do'.

In an interview with Christine Leigh March, Galloway has said

Simply for a woman to write as a woman, to be as honest about it as possible, is a statement; not falling into conventions and assuming guy stuff is 'real' stuff and we're a frill, a fuck or a boring bit that does housework and raises your kids around the edge. That stuff is not round the edge! It's the fucking middle of everything. Deliberately pointing up that otherness, where what passes for normal has no bearing on you or ignores you—that fascinates me.[10]

Domesticity, if I can use the shorthand borrowed from Mary McGlynn, is at the heart of almost all Galloway's fiction. Women own the means of domestic production—and certainly food production—in the majority, if not all, of Galloway's work. The extent to which Galloway's women are able to hold things together on the domestic front is an important marker for their ability to hold it together in a wider sense. In *Clara* there is delegation of household tasks to housemaids but it is still clearly the central women's role to oversee the running of the households.

Despite her domestic prowess, home life is difficult for Clara Schumann. Even in his more cheerful moments, Robert finds difficulty in expressing his feelings to Clara:

> That he loved her as only a husband can love went without saying. Almost completely without saying. Surely she knew? he thought to himself. Surely—surely she did not. Why else would she come, worried and white-faced sometimes, looking for reassurance, for the *words*. And the words— the tender words he had so often asked for himself in letters too—would not come. They lumped in his throat, refusing to be spoken and, truth to tell, he did not fight much to make it otherwise. (pp. 228–9)

But still she gets by. She is heartbroken—for example when she finds and reads an allegorical tale penned by Robert with the underlying message that love alone can never be enough—but she gets by.

Galloway describes the 'silences raddling the life' as 'The place, in other words, where [Clara] joins the rest of us in dealing with the everyday moral, financial and emotional struggles we call 'getting by'. In this way she is the model of how a woman can live life serving her friends and families and also serve her own talents and ambitions.' (p. 3)

I'm not entirely comfortable about adopting Clara as a role model. The novel certainly identifies plenty of occasions on which she is concerned with the service of her friends and especially her family—even to the extent of repairing relations with her father. But I remain unconvinced about the extent to which she also served her own talents and ambitions. In the same article,

---

10. Christie Leigh March, Interview with Janice Galloway, *Edinburgh Review 101—Exchanges*. Edinburgh: EUP, 1999.

Galloway herself describes Clara's silences and piano playing as 'survival tools'—hardly the same as serving talent. While it is clear from the novel that Clara gains considerable pleasure in performing, the novel also describes the international concert tours as, essentially, a means to bring money into the Schumann household. An initial exception is the first public performance she gives as Clara *Schumann*. It is Mendelssohn's idea that she and Robert should perform a joint concert—she playing his compositions—not to earn money directly, but as a benefit for the orchestra pension fund. It also has the happy benefit for Clara of buying her some practice time at the piano. Clara's performance raises the roof and 'for the first time since she was a child, it seemed, a concert was all pleasure, all reward.' (p. 208) But Robert is not so elated. At the end of the concert, she finds him hidden behind the orchestra curtain, apparently unmoved at the first public performance of his own work and anxious simply to go home. In a direct mirroring of Robert's inability to actually tell Clara he loves her, Clara tries to think how moved he must feel but

> … she did not know what to say. She picked words badly, could not describe how the things he had written made her feel. But he knew that. Surely he knew that. (p. 209)

For his part

> … he let his shoulders drop. Thank heaven, he said. I have been waiting an eternity. Come, *Clärchen.* Fetch your coat. (p. 209)

After the birth of their first child, Clara notices that her concert dresses don't fit her in the same way. But Robert points out that 'there was no immediate demand for concert dresses… She might sew, a good domestic occupation.' In a direct parallel with Joy Stone in *The Trick,* Clara dreams that she does not exist. In Clara's dream, it is Mendelssohn who is claiming 'he knew of no *Frau Schumann the pianist*, there was no such person at all.' (p. 219)

Frau Schumann *the composer* isn't even mentioned.

And yet she refuses to be swayed too far from getting by, from making sure that she'll always 'do'. As I've already noted, she is not dependent on the men in her life to help her do so. She learns to survive on her own, despite her father's best efforts to make her completely dependent on him, and Robert Schumann's illness, which has the effect of his becoming almost completely dependent on her.

Ali Smith has acknowledged that in *The Trick is to Keep Breathing*, Galloway '...goes where no man, except perhaps Gray in *1982, Janine*, has stylistically gone before, deep into representing the psyche of someone— importantly a woman in her case—whose world and self are falling to bits.'[11] In *Clara*, it is Robert Schumann who falls to bits, repeatedly, and Galloway movingly recounts each occasion.

Later in the same article, however, Smith criticises Galloway's technical and stylistic innovations, describing her fiction as 'peculiarly dated'. She says:

> ... looking at it now Galloway's fiction seems peculiarly dated in a way, already it has a late-eighties-Scottish-dirty-realism tag on it. Even the post-modern experiment and form games in her work, things which suggested freedom of form at the time, now look stylistically *of* a time, like the membership badge of a club of an era that's passing. As a writer Galloway seems shackled to a lot of things in *Blood* and *The Trick*... to an expected formal experimentation, and to this as-yet-unsolved problem in her work of gender identity, the paradox of the woman writing fiercely and bleakly at once about how gender silences you, takes away your language.

To deal with the last point first, I see no paradox in Galloway writing as eloquently and vividly as she does on the topic of women being silenced. There is more than one way to silence a lamb. In *Clara*, as in her other work, Galloway highlights the social and domestic circumstances that make it harder for women to speak out or to achieve their own ambitions. But *Clara* also emphasises the fact that even when women's achievements are considerable, if they are not valued, this in itself is a form of silencing. Those who would, however unintentionally, dismiss Galloway's work as 'women's writing'—like those who identify Clara's 'lumpy Saxon accent'—could be considered to be fulfilling a silencing role. It doesn't matter how fierce and bleak the prose, if all the audience hears (or is encouraged to hear) is a little lamb, bleating.

Smith's view of Galloway's work as dated contrasts sharply with the critical perspectives of Glenda Norquay and Mary McGlynn, both of whom clearly link her technical approach with the narrative content of her work.[12]

---

11. Ali Smith, 'Four Success Stories', *Chapman—the Woman's Forum*, No. 74–5, Autumn/ Winter 1993. Edinburgh: Chapman Publishing

McGlynn has written that 'Galloway's formal choices are… revealed to have a logic within the text; rather than experimentation for its own sake' (p. 4). This is undoubtedly true of *Clara*. In addition to the use of stylistic forms that will be very familiar to a Galloway audience—text set out across the page, the use of block capitals to lend emphasis, the inclusion of lists—*Clara* also introduces the reader to the language and symbolism of music. Music is represented both through the use of rhythm, pace and sentence sound in the text, and through the inclusion of musical notation.

In one particularly moving section, Galloway describes Robert Schumann's struggle with the intensity of feeling he has for the young Clara during one of his early periods of exile from the Wieck household. He hasn't received a reply to any letters from Clara for some time. He does not know that Clara's father has found and kept his letters, but only after reading them aloud 'articulating each [word] as though it belonged to a foreign language' (p. 123).

Robert attempts to dissipate the emotion and frustration he feels by composing—melodies based around five notes intended to spell out her name:

His fingers shook. He watched them till they stopped, then made coffee, very black, drank two sobering cups. Then he went back to his piano. He recharged his pen. C-L-A-R-A he wrote. C-L-A-R-A He had work to do. C-L-A-R-A Another piece to write. **C-L-A-R-A** Another, another. **C-L-A-R-A** Pieces stuffed with her **C-L-A-R-A** alive with her **C-L-A-R-A** roaring her

name (pp. 125–7)

Here the final climactic word ('name') appears printed across two pages. It

12. 'Janice Galloway's Novels: Fraudulent Mooching', *Contemporary Scottish Woman Writers.* Edinburgh University Press, 2000.

is possible to identify this passage as representing a climax of a physical, rather than strictly musical, kind. However, I do believe it may be interpreted entirely musically, mimicking the build up of a simple melody, perhaps sung by a solo voice, leading ultimately to the kind of crescendo created by a full orchestra.

One of the most immediately striking features of Galloway's work is her typographical innovation, the way she uses typeface and the position of words on the page to emphasise and elucidate meaning. While it is possible to imagine *Clara* minus the creative visual techniques in a way that it is hard to imagine *The Trick is to Keep Breathing* existing without them, I strongly believe that *Clara* is much the richer for their inclusion. The visual impact of *Clara* adds considerably to the overall experience of the novel. Bringing music into the text creates a linkage between the reader and the characters, permitting the characters to express themselves fully to the reader in their most eloquent form. Another effect of the passage I have quoted, relating to Robert's composing, is to give the reader an immediate sense of what it might be like to be a composer, to have your own tunes playing in your head, with no escape, no off switch. Galloway uses these textual innovations as another tool to help bring the message of her work closer to home.

As I have already noted, *Clara* is a novel about part of the life of Clara Wieck Schumann—a single song-cycle's-worth. The book concludes, not at the end of Clara's life, but when Robert Schumann dies. The message is clear: Clara had no life beyond these two men who oppressed her. But we know this is not true—we know this by conducting a little research of our own, for example to check that Clara Schumann outlived her husband by 40 years (and, in fact, survived a number of her own children). But we might guess something like this from the novel itself and the extent to which it conveys Clara's strength of character, her ability to get by.

The sheer irritating untoldness of the rest of her life is annoying for the reader who is left with so many questions at the end of the novel. This is an almighty ellipsis—of epic, black hole proportions—but it is no oversight. This is a lesson. It reminds us how little popular history has let us know about Clara Wieck Schumann. The fame she experienced in her lifetime has long since been eclipsed by that of her husband. Her compositions are seldom played. If we have heard of her at all it is most likely as the wife of Robert Schumann; her life expressed for posterity in relation to someone she was not.

In discussing *Clara,* Galloway has written:

History works against the accomplishments of most of us… and against the truer accomplishments and priorities of women especially. Women prioritise differently, although they know their achievement will be judged as harshly as a man's. And in this, writing about Clara was not merely writing about Clara at all. It was writing about the process of creativity from another perspective—the female creator's perspective.

Clara is a novel about silences. By ending the novel with Robert's death, Galloway silences Clara Wieck Schumann. In doing so, Galloway permits the silence of women throughout history to speak.

Coda

I create in the twilight hours, the edges of my life—and not just my own but the lives of those around me. I write in time stolen from other places: days taken off paid work while my daughter attends nursery; during the evenings while she sleeps (and when I'm not catching up on work, domestic and paid). During the night while others sleep, I steal hours from myself, rob them from my own sleep bank. And I'm lucky: I have a supportive partner where supportive equals non-obstructive individual who takes a share of the domestic tasks.

I collect my daughter from nursery. It's song time, accompanied by much laughter and shouting. I can hear my little girl before I see her. She's giggling, shouting '*I* sing it! *I* sing it!' And she does, unashamedly as any two-year old. She may not have the tune quite right, some of the words are in the wrong order, but it's her voice and she's singing.

Repeat to fade

Mmm…

Mastication, Men, Madness and Magazines:
Joy Stone meets Bridget Jones

Sharon Norris

Imagine, for a moment, the unthinkable. Joy Stone, the (anti-) heroine of Janice Galloway's first novel, *The Trick is to Keep Breathing* is sitting on a bench, waiting for someone. Joy is immaculately turned out, having spent much of the previous evening deciding on the appropriate dress, make-up. Her companion, whom she has read about but never actually met, has also spent time on her appearance, but to little effect. She is ten minutes late when she finally falls out of a taxi, her skirt tucked into her knickers. It's Bridget Jones.

Joy shakes hands. Says little. Observes all.

The two women go to a bar and order drinks—gin perhaps (a favourite of both), or maybe a bottle of Chardonnay. A love of alcohol is one thing, at least, they have in common. But thereafter… What on earth would they find to talk about?

If such a meeting seems unlikely, then so too must the project of this article—which is, to compare *The Trick is to Keep Breathing*, a novel which deals with death and depression, with Helen Fielding's twentieth century comedy of manners, *Bridget Jones's Diary*. However, as I hope to demonstrate here, there are in fact many, if unexpected, points of contact between the two novels.[1]

There are three key areas where I believe a comparison can most usefully be made: the novels' relation to pre-existing traditions; the use of ironic humour; and common subject matter.

The publication, in 1996, of *Bridget Jones's Diary* saw Helen Fielding hailed as having given birth to a whole new literary genre—chick lit. The novel started life as a column in *The Independent*; however, when Fielding was approached to write a book based on the latter she opted to structure this around the basic framework of *Pride and Prejudice*.

In addition to this obvious link with Austen, however, I believe that Fielding, in *Bridget Jones's Diary*, can also be seen to share common literary ground with her namesake, *Henry* Fielding,[2] in the rambunctiousness of both her heroine and of her writing style. This link extends to the astute commentary on the social mores of the day that both novels offer. Perhaps a more obvious and important link with the eighteenth century novel is the book's use of diary form, which links it with the epistolary novel especially popular during that era. Historically, one notable feature of the latter was its frequent use of neologisms, and *Bridget Jones's Diary* is no exception. 'Smug Marrieds', 'fuckwittage' and, most important of all, 'Singleton' are all now part of our common vocabulary.

Joy, the central character in Galloway's novel, can be read as a variation on the nineteenth century novel's 'mad woman in the attic'. However, *The Trick is to Keep Breathing* can also be linked to more recent female narratives about mental illness, as well as to the traditions of the Postmodern novel.

If we are to consider Galloway's novel as '*proto*-chick lit', it is important, first of all, to establish the defining characteristics of chick lit itself. There is some debate as to how far back the genre can trace its origins. If we were to define chick lit simply as fiction written primarily by women and from a female perspective, and which deals with women's lives as they are lived then Jane Austen's work would easily qualify. If we were to jettison the female author as pre-requisite, then George Gissing's *The Odd Women* (1883) might also pass. Nevertheless, chick lit is most often viewed as a genre of the 1990s, with chick lit novels, characteristically, being introspective, intimate and

---

1. All quotations henceforth are from Galloway, J (1991), *The Trick is to Keep Breathing*, London: Minerva, and Fielding, H (1997), *Bridget Jones's Diary*, London: Picador.
2. Henry Fielding, of course, famously parodied Richardson's epistolary novel, *Pamela*, in *Shamela*.

confiding, and very often written in the first person. Here we can see more parallels with the eighteenth century novel and with those of Samuel Richardson in particular. We can also see some major points of contact between chick lit in general and *The Trick is to Keep Breathing*, and insofar as each of these points applies to *Bridget Jones's Diary*, between Fielding's novel and Galloway's.

Although chick lit is most often viewed as a comic genre, there are several chick lit authors, most notably Marian Keyes, whose work deals with darker subject matter.[3] One could argue then that Galloway's novel perhaps would be most usefully viewed against those more serious examples of the species. Nevertheless, it in is Galloway's use of humour, I believe, that we can see a particularly significant link between *The Trick is to Keep Breathing* and *Bridget Jones's Diary*.

As a conscious re-working of Austen, it is perhaps only to be expected that Fielding's novel, and its sequel, *Bridget Jones: The Edge of Reason* (Picador, 2000) should be heavily ironic. However, comic irony is also a key feature of Galloway's novel, and despite its ostensibly bleak subject matter, *The Trick is to Keep Breathing* is often achingly funny. Narrative technique and ironic humour are ideally matched here, for where the former involves a visiting and re-visiting of the same incidents, with a little more detail given each time, ironic humour allows Joy simultaneously to acknowledge *and* distance herself (and the reader) from painful events. It also allows for a much more readable novel than one might have expected. That said, Joy's ability always to 'see the joke', like many aspects of this novel, is ambiguous, in that it also operates potentially as means for self-subversion.

Humour also has a more generally subversive intent here. It allows Galloway to challenge expectations and received norms, most obviously as regards the appropriateness of humour in a novel dealing with depression. Within the world of the book, Galloway, through Joy, uses humour to challenge, *inter alia*, female social roles and the attitude of mental health professionals—both of which are seen to play a significant part in Joy's illness.

Chick lit's use of humour can also be seen to be subversive, and doubly so. Firstly, the very *fact* of women writing in a humorous way, and within the context of a genre written almost exclusively by and for women writers,

---

3.   There has been a debate as to as to whether or not recent and more 'mature' novels by writers usually linked with the genre *are* actually chick lit proper, or rather an entirely new genre, variously referred to as 'hen lit', or 'mum lit'.

could, in itself, be said to be 'oppositional'. Secondly, the fact that novels such as *Bridget Jones's Diary* use humour to tackle issues such as female social roles and the treatment of women in the workplace is also subversive, not least of all because it reflects a willingness to subvert even the established traditions and expectations set up by earlier female writers. For where novelists such as Fay Weldon and, to a degree, Doris Lessing, can be seen to have covered some of the same ground, chick lit favours humour over anger as its dominant mode.

To the extent that both these novels can be said to use humour subversively, we can trace not only a further link between Fielding and Austen, but also a link between Galloway and Austen. In his 1940 essay, 'Regulated Hatred', D. W. Harding argued that Austen was infinitely more subversive than most critics of her work hitherto had recognised. He writes that:

> ...her books are, as she meant them to be, read and enjoyed by precisely the sort of people whom she disliked; she is a literary classic of the society which attitudes like hers, held widely enough, would undermine.[4]

Austen's technique of 'slipping' what is essentially rather scathing criticism of her social milieu into speeches made by sympathetic characters, says Harding, is deliberate. She chose to write in this way because, for all their shortcomings, she needed the very people she criticised, and did not want to alienate them entirely. At the same time, while she genuinely appreciated the achievements of her society, she recognised her own precarious position within it.

It strikes me that a similar thing is going on in *The Trick is to Keep Breathing*. Galloway's criticisms of society, and, in particular, of female social roles, may be more overt than Austen's. Nevertheless, like Austen, she too frequently uses ironic humour to make her point. Within the context of a critique of the mental health establishment, for example, the effect is unsettling, and the criticism itself all the more trenchant. Harding's comments on Austen's relation to society and its norms, furthermore, could just as easily be applied to Joy, and perhaps, by extension, to Galloway

---

4. Harding, D. W. (1940), 'Regulated Hatred; An Aspect of the work of Jane Austen', in *Scrutiny*, (D. W. Harding, L C. Knight and F. R. Leavis, eds.), Vol. III, no. 4, March 1940, p.347.

herself: '...[she] knew that her real existence depended on resisting many of the values they implied.'[5]

Fielding's use of ironic humour allows her novel, like Austen's work, to be understood at different levels. This can be seen to apply, among other things, to her various references to feminism in *Bridget Jones's Diary*.

Despite chick lit's popularity, it tends to be critically disparaged, and in this respect it is similar to romantic fiction, which also has a primarily female readership. It is this lowly critical status that perhaps makes a comparison between Fielding's novel and *The Trick is to Keep Breathing* seem like something of an insult to the latter. However, Bridget Fowler's admittedly somewhat double-edged defence of romantic fiction could also be said to apply here:

> ...if archaeologists can discover valuable materials for reconstructing
> societies from prehistoric middens, even the most formulaic romance
> may reveal important clues to both human needs and the existing social
> relations within which they are expressed.[6]

It would be remiss for any study of Galloway's work to overlook its feminism, given the author's own well-documented views on the subject. However, the issue of feminism is particularly relevant here, both given the extent to which Joy's journey back to health is seen to involve a resistance to specific forms of female stereotyping, and also since Fielding herself has acknowledged that her novel has often been criticised by feminists for being 'regressive'. Notwithstanding this, as I hope to show, *Bridget Jones's Diary* can be read as 'post-feminist'. For her part, Galloway is on record as having challenged the notion that we live in a 'post-feminist era'.[7]

It is illuminating to compare Fielding and Galloway's feminism in these two books in relation to Rosalind Coward's work on feminism and popular culture. *Female Desire*,[8] published in 1984, is a collection of essays on the various sources of pleasure afforded to women by popular culture. These include food, magazines, horoscopes, and popular fiction. Although there have been other more detailed studies, both before and since, which have

5.   Ibid., p.351.
6.   Fowler, B (1991), *The Alienated Reader: Women and Popular Romantic Literature in the Twentieth Century*, Hemel Hempstead: Harvester Wheatsheaf, p.1.
7.   See Bowditch, G (2002), 'Still angry after all these years', *The Sunday Times*, 23rd June.
8.   Coward, R (1984), *Female Desire*, London: Paladin.

focused on some of these aspects, most notably the studies of women's magazines conducted by Marjorie Ferguson[9] and Janice Winship, Coward's study is particularly relevant here given the breadth of its scope.

However, Winship offers a useful guide as to how we should understand the term 'post-feminist' not as an acknowledgement that the feminist agenda has won the day, rather:

> [it] suggests that feminism no longer has a simple coherence around a set of easily defined principles… but instead is a much richer, more diverse and contradictory mix than it ever was in the 1970s.[10]

'Female desire', Rosalind Coward argues, 'is courted with the promise of future perfection', despite the fact that these ideals 'don't actually exist, except as photographic techniques or as elaborate fantasies'.[11] Coward's thesis is that women participate in certain aspects of popular culture at a cost. This can include loss of identity, opportunity, and, ultimately, of any prospect of happiness—since female desire for these pursuits is exposed, in essence, as 'dissatisfaction recast'. Worse still, any pleasure gained invariably generates guilt—'our speciality', as Coward calls it (p. 14).

The main characters' desperate attempts both to live up to 'ideals' and to negotiate the twin poles of the pleasure/guilt axis can be seen to be a characteristic feature in both novels here. However, one might say that while with Bridget it's pleasure that gains the upper hand, with Joy it's guilt.

One further area of comparison between these two books in respect of their narrative form is their recurrent use of *leitmotifs*. There is a particularly interesting link in the fact that both books use *leitmotifs* related to the letter 'm'. Formal and thematic *leitmotif* come together in Galloway's use of the initial 'M' to link the names of the two people Joy loves, or has loved, most— her best friend, Marianne, and her dead lover, Michael. However, the initial 'M' also links them to the two most loathed characters in the book—Joy's Mother, now also dead, and her sister, Myra.

Interestingly, ambiguity can also be seen in *Bridget Jones's Diary* in relation to the use of 'm'. Here 'Mmm' (and the marginally more expansive 'Mmmm') appears both as an expression of desire—sexual, and for food—and to

---

9.   Ferguson, M (1983), *Forever Feminine: Women's Magazines and the Cult of Femininity*, London: Heinemann.
10.   Winship, J (1987), *Inside Women's Magazines*, London: Pandora, p. 149.
11.   Coward, (op. cit.), p. 13.

indicate hesitancy. This ambiguity is rare in a novel that is almost exclusively 'positive'.

Mastication—food and its consumption

I want now to appropriate 'm', as a *leitmotif* of sorts, in order to examine four key themes that link these two novels. It has been said of Janice Galloway she 'doesn't write about, but through, feminism'.[12] I propose to write, as it were, 'through' these particular 'm's to reveal, *inter alia*, the extent to which feminism functions as a prism for Galloway.

Food lies very firmly on Coward's pleasure/guilt axis, and for both Joy and Bridget, food and the eating of it are central pre-occupations. Food is the desired object, however both women strive to deny themselves—with varying degrees of success. Predictably, it is Joy who shows the greater self-discipline, and of the two is the more likely to starve herself to death than be eaten by any Alsatian. The refusal to eat however carries extra 'weight' in *The Trick is to Keep Breathing*, in that it is no less than a refusal of life itself. Thus although both women are prepared to deny themselves food, it is only Joy who regularly makes herself vomit.

Both women are also shown bingeing—in Bridget's case with Newtonian predictability. Bridget's refusal of food, however, although contradictory, is much more straightforward than Joy's. She is caught on the horns of what is framed as an essentially female dilemma. Although she craves food, she also craves the 'ideal' (i.e. slim) body. The irony here, however, is that her perpetual calorie-counting ultimately proves not only useless, but counter-productive. Not only does she invariably end up at the same weight, when she does eventually go on a diet, the general consensus is that she looked better before.

Food has an altogether more complex role to play in Galloway's novel. Many of the key events here are detailed with reference to food. Both the beginning and end of Joy's relationship with former boyfriend, Paul, is detailed in relation to food. They have their first date in a café, and finally split up after an argument over whether he needs Joy to cook for him. Paul storms out, eventually returning to the house with: 'A Chinese take-away. For one' (p. 43). Weighty as the theme of food is here, it also comes laden with

---

12. See Burgess, M (1998), *Imagine a City: Glasgow in Fiction,* Glendaruel: Argyll Publishing, p. 311.

characteristic comic irony. Towards the end of the novel, Joy goes out for a 'therapeutic dinner with wine' with fellow-patients from the psychiatric hospital. However, given that the majority are in hospital due to problems related either to food or alcohol, the therapeutic potential of this evening is seen to be questionable (p. 160).

Food has a multi-layered significance in this novel. For Ellen, Marianne's mother, food represents both 'love' and 'medicine' (p. 85), and is something of an obsession. This enables Joy to use the all-too-plausible excuse that she is 'having a meal with Ellen' (p. 93) to avoid going out (for a meal) with Tony, her married boss from the bookies' shop where she works on Saturdays. Elsewhere food takes on sexual connotations, such as in Joy's description of the other patients' 'near-sexual thrill with the food' in the hospital (p. 139).

Joy's refusal to eat is both a means of exerting some control over her life, and an expression of self-loathing—for although she starves herself, she still has an appetite (p. 76). Tony and others encourage Joy to 'eat more', but with Tony in particular Joy appears to see this as an attempt at control which must be resisted. Furthermore, it misses the point. Joy doesn't want to live, so why eat?

Joy's ambivalence towards food further underlines the masochistic impulse in her purchase of women's magazines, for she buys these, in part, for recipes for food that she would never allow herself to eat. Nonetheless, the magazines themselves are seen to present conflicting ideals of women—as cooks and (implicit) consumers of exceptional meals, *and* possessors of slim and sexy bodies. Joy's 'ULTIMATE DIET' (p. 85) gives a sardonic twist to this, as it is no less than a recipe for starvation.

While Joy *can* cook, and appears to enjoy it, Bridget 'thinks big' in the kitchen but inevitably ends up with her feet in the mashed potatoes. It is here that some interesting questions emerge in relation to the two writers' feminism (or post-feminism). In a 1999 interview, Fielding commented that Bridget's desire to impress in the kitchen is a response to women's perceived need to be 'perfect' in all areas. She remarks, tellingly, of the disastrous consequences of Bridget's cooking that:

> Women like that because instead of stressing out about our imperfections, we can share a laugh at them.[13]

---

13. 'Helen Fielding Is Not Bridget Jones', (interview with Dave Weich). www.powells.com/authors/fielding.html

Even if Joy *does* like cooking, we might question whether or not this is due to the genuine pleasure it affords, or to an unconscious desire to conform to a particular female stereotype. The question arises then as to which of the two women is the more 'liberated'—Joy who is all culinary competence, or Bridget who aspires to this but ultimately is happy to have other people take over in the kitchen.

Men

It is in examining their treatment of men that one might reasonably expect the feminist credentials of these two writers to become most evident. However, all is not as it appears, and the question of which of the two novels is the more 'regressive' arises once more.

On the surface at least, Fielding's heroine again seems to be the more conservative. Men are fantasised about in relation to shared trips to the supermarket or idyllic mini-breaks. Even if they are not given sole responsibility for sex, men *are* awarded full responsibility for matters ethical. Bridget's boyfriend, Mark Darcy, is a human rights barrister, and this combination of intelligence and ethical awareness is seen to make him especially attractive. The intelligence/ethics combination can also be seen in the character of O'Rourke,[14] the heroine's boyfriend in Fielding's first novel, *Cause Celeb*. This would seem to suggest that Fielding's women prefer their male counterparts to 'do their ethics' for them.

In *The Trick is to Keep Breathing*, Joy acknowledges that men have always represented 'better things' (p. 56). Her expectations of men, implicit in her relationships with them, are two-fold: they are there for emotional support, and to provide physical, though not necessarily sexual, comfort. This applies to lovers as well as to male friends. When the balance of these two elements is lost, for example with Tony, who pushes the physical side but is emotionally insensitive, Joy recoils.

Joy's relationships with men are all seen to be complicated in one way or another. With Tony in particular, she seems to oscillate between 'pliant' and 'resistant'. Tony has 'never met anyone' like Joy. Unfortunately, Joy finds him all too predictable. As manager of the bookies', Tony has taken on the trappings of a particularly working class definition of 'responsibility'. The

---

14. Fielding, H (1995), *Cause Celeb*, London: Picador.

same age as Joy, he looks and dresses older than his years. However, class and education are significant factors here. Where Joy and Michael swap musical references and read the Sunday broadsheets, she and Tony have no common intellectual reference points. What complicates this is that Joy nonetheless seems ready to accept, at least on occasion, that the fact of Tony's being a man somehow overrides all else.

Throughout the novel, the rules governing the relative social expectations for men and women are shown to be fraught with double standards, as an ironic footnote indicates:

> *'Love/Emotion = embarrassment: Scots equation. Exceptions are when roaring drunk or watching football. Men do rather better out of this loophole'* (p. 82, emphasis in original).

That said, Joy herself is not above double standards. Having had a relationship with Michael, a 'Married Man', she then takes Tony to task about *his* wife as he attempts to seduce her. Nevertheless, she still sleeps with him. Furthermore, Joy arguably shows a naïveté in her inability fully to understand either Michael's wife's hostility towards her or that of certain sections of the local community. There is also an implicit double standard in her relationship with David, originally a pupil at the school where Joy works, who is ten years younger than she is. If Tony is seen as a predatory man taking advantage of Joy's vulnerability, is she not also a predatory woman taking advantage of David's youth? She starts the affair with David, moreover, while she is still living with Paul.

In both novels, the lack of a man has wider social significance. It is not just the shock of personal grief that Joy has to deal with when Michael dies, but the sense of social dislocation that accompanies this. To that extent, Joy could be seen as a 'Singleton'. She also has her own 'Smug Married' to contend with, in Nancy, the hospital OT, who is both incredulous and patronising when she hears that Joy has never been married (p. 141).

Sex is one area where an interesting comparison can be made between the characters, for where Bridget mainly fantasises about it, Joy is actually 'shagging'. Joy is thus, ironically, the bad 'good' girl, while Bridget, the 'girl-about-town', is comparatively restrained. While this might seem to indicate a sexual conservatism, it is something else. For all her apparent neuroses, Bridget has self-respect. Joy's sexual 'liberation' is, in fact, nothing of the sort. It is rooted in misery and proceeds from need, though not always sexual need. Even when it is, it is not always her own.

There is an additional ironic 'double standard' in Galloway's novel in that, despite illness and bereavement, the central character still worries about her appearance when she is due at the bookies' shop, because she'll be working with men (p.30). She also prays that a stranger she hears approaching her house isn't a man, because she looks so bad (p.210). Even if this irony is intended, Gillian Bowditch, in her interview with Galloway cited above nevertheless makes a similar observation in respect of the author herself: 'It is hard to associate this staunchly feminist dogma with Galloway in her pastel cardigan and floaty skirt…'[15] Are we, after all, in 'the post-feminist era'—or is this just a blind spot?

Madness

It is in consideration of their treatment of madness that the comparison between these two novels begins to come unstuck—for here we are forced to acknowledge that we are not comparing like with like. If Daniel Cleaver initially is Bridget's 'soi-disant' boyfriend, then madness too, insofar as it appears in Bridget's diary, is only 'soi-disant'. Insofar as any of the characters could be said to be mentally unbalanced, this is of the nature of neurosis, rather than psychosis. In Galloway's novel, by contrast, genuine clinical madness is always lurking in the background as a possible outcome for Joy.

Fielding milks the tension between the implicitly understood clinical definition of 'madness', and the common parlance sense in which the word is understood here, for comic effect.[16] Characters with actual mental illness do appear in both Bridget Jones books, and interestingly, in each case, schizophrenia is the 'illness of choice'.[17] In neither instance, however, is this dealt with in any way 'seriously'. Although it could be argued that this is understandable given the context, nevertheless, is has to be seen as a deliberate choice on the part of the author. It is not that Fielding is incapable of writing about darker topics, even within the context of a comic novel, as

---

15. Bowditch, op. cit.
16. 'Paranoid' and 'obsessive', which recur throughout the novel, are used in a similar way, and the tension between the clinical and common parlance understandings of 'madness' also underlie the title of the second Bridget Jones book.
17. Bridget's granny is said to have 'turned schizophrenic' in the first book, while in the second Bridget thinks Mark Darcy must be gay after finding the housekeeper's schizophrenic son in her boyfriend's bed.

Cause Celeb demonstrates. Nor, as we have seen, is chick lit as a genre unable to sustain more serious subject matter. Perhaps what this *does* indicate is both Fielding's, and society as a whole's, unease about mental illness. Nevertheless, Galloway too raises issues in respect of ambivalence towards madness.

The Trick is to Keep Breathing can be seen as part of a tradition of narratives by women, often written in the first person, which deal with mental illness.[18] In many of these, a recurrent issue is the extent to which the female characters' madness is socially constructed and directly related to the pressures of conforming to traditional gender roles. In Galloway's novel, although Joy's depression is seen to be related to specific events in her past, nevertheless her journey to sanity involves her having to swim against a tide of gender-related expectations—for example that she will be 'good' (p. 81, pp. 137–8), not 'disappoint' (p. 182), and be prepared to wait for things to get better (p. 193). All of these are presented as 'what women do'.

Notwithstanding the latter, the credible presentation of mental illness here raises issues in respect of that branch of feminist thought which sees female madness as something to be welcomed—an empowered response to male-prescribed 'norms'.[19] In the real world however, this idealisation of mental illness surely offers little comfort to any woman in the throes of psychosis.

Ironically, although there appears to be a very different relationship between mental illness and humour from one narrative to the other, there *is* a connection. If Fielding initially exploits the tension between the clinical and common parlance definitions of 'madness' for comic effect, her unease with the topic ultimately reveals itself where she resorts to treating madness *per se* as a source of comedy. In *The Trick is to Keep Breathing*, it is Galloway's recognition of this broader societal unease with mental illness, which she exploits to wickedly comic effect. Joy, furthermore, is in a position of power here, as is Galloway, implicitly, in being able to laugh from the perspective of 'insider'.

---

18. E.g. Sylvia Plath's *The Bell Jar*, Veronica Hull's *The Monkey Puzzle*, and Jean Rhys's *Wide Sargasso Sea*.
19. '…the hysteric is… the typical woman in all her force'. Cixous, H. and Clement, C. (1986), *The Newly Born Woman*, translated by Betsy Wing, introduction by Sandra Gilbert. Manchester: Manchester University Press.

Magazines (and other reading material)

One particularly fruitful area of comparison between Joy and Bridget is their respective reading habits. Joy, we are told, reads to find 'truth', and reads 'everything', from 'tins in supermarkets' and 'leaflets that come through the door' (p. 37) to *Fat is a Feminist Issue* (p. 195). Bridget, who initially works in publishing, has similarly catholic tastes. Both women, however, have preferred reading material—for Bridget this is self-help books, for Joy, glossy magazines.

The magazines fall firmly on Coward's pleasure/guilt axis. They offer advice—for example, on how not to get raped (p. 130)—and reassurance—that it's 'fairly common' to grieve for Michael in this way (p. 83). They even, potentially, offer approval![20] On the other hand, as indicated above, they further fuel Joy's love/hate relationship with food. They are also a major source of irony, and this is achieved partially through Joy's adoption of 'magazine-speak' in her narrative, and partially through the ironic juxtaposition of magazine 'excerpts' with traumatic events from Joy's life. They thus offer an ironic commentary. Nowhere is this more apparent than in the narrative's use of horoscopes. Joy, for example, tries to convince herself that Michael isn't dead by a simple act of rationalising, based on her having read his horoscope. She asks:

> How could he be having a difficult phase with money if he was dead. (p. 83)

In *Female Desire*,[21] Rosalind Coward argues that the spheres of action covered by horoscopes are actually very limited, and she relates this, in turn, to Roland Barthes' observation in *Mythologies*,[22] that horoscopes merely reflect 'the social reality of the group producing them'. Thus, horoscopes, specifically, and magazines in general, can be seen both to reflect and endorse the existence of limited horizons for women. Joy, recognising that they are not helping her recovery, eventually concludes that she has to 'stop reading these fucking magazines' (p. 223), but the magazines have one final ironic gift to bestow.

---

20. Of the way Joy and Michael discuss their living arrangements after he has left his wife, 'The magazines would have approved like hell', says Joy (p. 65).
21. 'Affairs of the Heart are Well-aspected', Coward (op. cit.), pp. 218–23.
22. Barthes, R (1973), *Mythologies*, London: Paladin.

Books and other reading material also play an important ironic role in Fielding's novel. Certain books occur and recur as ironic *leitmotifs*, in particular, *Backlash*, Susan Faludi's critique of institutionalised anti-female prejudice, and Ben Okri's Booker-winning novel, *The Famished Road*. The use of Faludi's book as *leitmotif*, for those alert to its significance, can be seen as Fielding poking fun at a certain strand of feminism thought, and at certain types of response to this—such as that of Bridget's would-be 'strident feminist' friend, Sharon.

What the Faludi and Okri books also have in common is that they are both presented here as 'trophy books'. That is, although Bridget has read neither, she thinks she ought to, both because they are understood to be 'important', and because everyone else has. Both of these reasons can be read as a desire on Bridget's part to connect with other people.[23]

Joy's magazines can also be seen to function as a potential bridge to the other 'you's addressed in the horoscopes and problem pages. Thus, despite their frequently negative influence, at one level at least the magazines are a positive source of pleasure for Joy, both in that she enjoys reading them *and* they afford her the possibility of 'belonging'.

Bridget's self-help books posses a similarly ambiguous status to that of Joy's magazines, in that they simultaneously offer advice and increase Bridget's sense of inadequacy. As with Joy's decision about the magazines, Bridget eventually resolves (in *Bridget Jones: The Edge of Reason*) to get rid of these books—and for similar reasons.

The similarities in Bridget's recourse to self-help books and Joy's to magazines can be read in a number of ways—for example, as a need to 'belong', *and* for quasi-spiritual guidance in a secular world. This perceived need for exemplars, and the fact that Bridget and Joy both turn to primarily female-oriented reading materials again raises questions about the feminist status of each novel. It also reflects back on one final 'm', which unites the two books.

As I have shown, the issue of feminism in each of these novels is closely interwoven with the treatment of the four 'm's discussed above. While the four themes are often presented ambivalently, it is the extent to which Bridget and Joy each *respond* to them in contradictory ways that is crucial.

---

23. For a fuller discussion on trophy books, see McCracken, S. (1998), *Pulp Fictions—Reading Popular Fictions*, Manchester: Manchester University Press, pp. 43–4.

Insofar as any conclusions can be inferred about Fielding and Galloway's feminism from the novels, these must be viewed properly in context. It is not just that the novels belong to two quite disparate genres. We must also acknowledge the marked differences in the social contexts of the two main characters.

Margaret Elphinstone appears to locate Galloway's novel within the tradition of female narratives concerned with the social construction of mental illness, when she comments that Joy, 'stuck in contemporary Ayrshire can go no further than madness'.[24] Joy's feminism must also be seen to be mediated and ultimately constrained, variously, by the influences of Calvinism, a male-dominated west of Scotland working class ethic, and, finally, by the specific legacies of family. In all of these contextual areas however Bridget can be said, relative to Joy at least, to belong to a 'culture of entitlement'—even as a woman. Thus, the two women's feminism(s) must be seen to exist in, and be determined by, the realm of the possible—noting that 'the possible' differs for each character.

The same might be said of the authors' feminism, and this has a particular relevance to the extent that either book can be said to be in any way autobiographical.[25] One additional factor, which may be significant, is the relative ages of the two writers and of their characters. The four-year age difference between Galloway and Fielding may not seem a lot. However, coupled with the factors listed above, and with the fact that the novels are set roughly a decade apart, the 'realm of the possible' for women might be said to have changed through time.

Nevertheless, if Galloway's novel is the more overtly feminist, the fact that the 'ideal' is still aspired to in *Bridget Jones's Diary*, despite the time lapse, would tend to suggest that feminism has had a limited impact. The fact, too, that Fielding's humour is regularly turned on feminism, for example in the ironic references to Faludi's book, and, more directly, in Bridget's comment to Sharon, that 'there is nothing so unattractive to a man as strident feminism' (p. 20), would seem only to confirm this. Fielding herself, in the interview

---

24. See Elphinstone, M (1997), 'Contemporary Feminist Fantasy in the Scottish Literary Tradition', *Tea and Leg Irons: New Feminist Readings from Scotland,* edited by Caroline Gonda, London: Open Letters, p. 48.

25. While Galloway acknowledges that *The Trick is to Keep Breathing* is related to events in her own life, she usually plays down the extent to which it is 'autobiography' as such. Fielding denies that she is Bridget Jones, but frequently admits to having 'shamelessly plundered' aspects of her own life for the character.

mentioned above, seems to reinforce this criticism, when she mentions this line as one of her 'favourites' in the novel.

Instead of seeing all this as 'regressive', it would be more accurate, I believe, to read it as evidence that Fielding at least believes in 'the post-feminist era'. While Bridget and Joy both aspire to female 'ideals', Bridget is far more tolerant of her faults (as are her readers) than Galloway's heroine. This, I think, reveals a certain underlying confidence, not only on Bridget's part, but ultimately also on Fielding's, that women's failure to match up to, or indeed properly address the 'ideal' is perfectly acceptable.

As for Joy, if her struggle to survive in the female realm of the possible is linked directly to her journey to recovery, the latter is shown to be not just a case of regaining her health. The one final 'm' which links *The Trick is to Keep Breathing* and *Bridget Jones's Diary* is that they can both be read as quests for 'meaning'—though what this signifies, and the extent to which this search is made explicit, varies greatly from one book to the other.

The search for meaning is central to Galloway's novel, and is made explicit through Joy's constant search for 'the point'. This very quest in itself, however, is shown to be problematic. She traces the origins of her depression back to her overwhelming need to make sense of the apparently random way terrible things happen, and her inability to do so, expressed in the novel as her 'minding'. Ironically, having recognised this, she then tries to rationalise even this, and entertains the notion that there may be a family predisposition to it—'hereditary minding'. For Joy, this, like the horoscopes, offers the welcome prospect of her being able to side-step any sense of personal responsibility, both for 'the way things are', and for changing them.

Joy originally envisages 'the point' as something which will either explain why bad things happen, or, alternatively, provide a bulwark against arbitrariness. However meaning is discovered to have only specific and not universal application. Furthermore, it exists, as does love (in Galloway's book of short stories), 'where you find it'. So too does truth, and here the magazines, a trashy self-help book, and even one of Tony's jokes (p. 173), are all seen to have a role to play in pointing Joy towards a new *modus vivendi*. Where Joy has previously traced the origins of her depression to events and situations that pre-date Michael's death, this new insight has the potential not only to banish her current depression, but also, to offer a whole new approach to life.

Galloway's novel then can be seen as Existentialist in that it involves both a search for 'Meaning' and an acknowledgement that there is, after all, only 'meaning'. Joy starts to recover when she begins to ask not 'why' but 'how' to live. The trick is, literally, 'to keep breathing'. This, I believe, calls into question the novel's status as a 'Postmodern narrative', for in its search for meaning, and both a narrative structure and thematic development which presuppose that resolution is possible, it is surely more accurate to see *The Trick is to Keep Breathing* as a Modernist novel, but one which employs Postmodern devices.

Given her shift in perspective, it is perhaps unfair to postulate any meeting between these two characters without first specifying whether we mean the Joy at the beginning, or the one who emerges at the end, of Galloway's novel. For although superficially nothing has changed, and Joy is seen, at both points, sitting alone at home, in fact *everything* has changed. To a degree, the same can also be said of Bridget; however, here, by contrast, the significant shift which precedes fulfilment of *her* quest appears to involve no more than a willingness to recognise that she is fine the way she is. Again, we might argue whether this makes Bridget more confidently 'post-feminist' or regressive.

Where Joy is forced to acknowledge that other people cannot 'love [her] into existence', Bridget's sense of meaning is shown to be intimately bound up in her relationships—with her friends and especially with Mark, who by the end of the novel seems likely to be a permanent fixture. Although in consciously following Austen, Fielding's hands are somewhat tied here, this can be seen as an endorsement of Fowler's re-statement of Ernst Bloch's observation,[26] that 'a happy ending, seen through but still defended' is a literary imperative. However, if Fielding's novel is essentially wish-fulfilment, so too (at one level), is Galloway's, given that Joy finds some meaning to her life after all.

As I hope I have demonstrated, to make a comparison of these two novels is neither to detract from Galloway's achievement in what remains a remarkable novel; nor is it to overstate Fielding's in the creation of Bridget Jones. The various points of contact between these two apparently disparate novels suggests not only that Coward and others are correct in their analyses of the way women relate to popular culture, but also that there are some fundamental similarities in the way women experience and negotiate their lives, and in how they construct their sense of identity.

So, perhaps we can assume that Joy and Bridget might have found something to talk about after all.

---

26. From *The Principle of Hope*. Quoted in Fowler (op. cit.), p.4.

A woman's guilt, a woman's violence
Self-destructive behaviour in *The Trick is to Keep Breathing*

Eve Lazovitz

Early on in Janice Galloway's *The Trick is to Keep Breathing*, Joy Stone says of her best friend's move to America, 'I couldn't believe she was going far: you never go too far on an island. Eventually you reach water' (Galloway 1994, 35). She says this because her own world ends where the coast of Great Britain meets the water. She cannot leave the land for unclear oceans where feet do not rest on the ground. She cannot even leave her own mind. Joy is trapped in a world of depression and grief, a world of repressed emotions and lurking thoughts, a world that is invisible to those around her. It is as if she herself is the island, separated from others by obscure waters, singled out and unable to swim.

Joy is haunted by feelings of hopelessness, fear, non-existence, and guilt. Her reaction to her lover Michael's drowning is typically female in that she wonders if she is to blame. *'He must have been under the water for ten minutes, maybe fifteen. The yellow bruise on his forehead and the two on the chest: hit his head on the bottom maybe. Did I have any reason to believe he did it on purpose? Any reason at all?'* (166). Waking up from a dream about him to find that he is not with her, Joy thinks to herself, *'My fault. I opened my eyes'* (152). This guilt mingles with the guilt she feels for having been a mistress rather than a wife, for being 'unwell,' for having emotions, for wasting people's time, for not being perfect, and for being womanly in some respects while distinctly unfeminine in others. This is the burden that sits alongside her sorrow, her anxiety and loneliness. It is the burden that weighs down on her, keeping her from swimming out into the uncharted waters that surround her, from dealing honestly and personally with her emotions.

Joy's self-destructive behaviour is a response to this burden, a response to the guilt that she has added to her grief and depression. Her anorexia, bulimia, alcoholism, and acts of self-mutilation serve many purposes in her life, both blatantly and subconsciously. They are acts of punishment, escape, control, and submission, as well as cries for help. Joy feels the burn of stomach acid in the throat and the sting of lemon juice on freshly cut fingers. She does this to combat the real pain she feels, the emotional pain that belittles the physical pain of her small acts of violence but is somehow easier to face because of them.

In the introduction to *Meantime: Looking Forward to the New Millennium*, Janice Galloway says the following about being a woman, being a woman in Scotland, and being a woman writer in Scotland:

> Scottish women have their own particular complications with writing and definition, complications which derive from the general problems of being a colonised nation. Then, that wee touch extra. Their sex. There is coping with that guilt of taking time off the concerns of national politics to get concerned with the sexual sort: that creeping fear it's somehow self-indulgent to be more concerned for one's womanness instead of one's Scottishness, one's working class heritage or whatever. Guilt here comes strong from the notion we're not backing up our menfolk and their 'real' concerns. Female concerns, like meat on the mother's plate, are extras after the man and the weans have been served (Galloway 1991, 5–6)

This female guilt that she discusses is not specifically that of an author who writes about women's concerns. It is a guilt felt by women who blame themselves for behaviour that can only be seen as natural and who take responsibility in that typically mothering way for that over which they have no control. It is a guilt that women feel because they are concerned about themselves, about the everyday occurrences of their ordinary lives, and it is a guilt felt because these occurrences are not acknowledged as important by society. Anaïs Nin, writer and feminist, says of woman that 'there is always that feeling which keeps her from growing. The feeling that if she grows she is going to impede someone else's growth and that her concern should be not to take too much space and not to expand… So woman carries many, many

126

burdens' (Nin 1975, 39).

Joy Stone carries many burdens, for she is not only the woman, but the 'other' woman. Her role is one not readily accepted by society, one that people ignore or pretend not to see. She is the woman who does not really count. During the special service for Michael held at school, Joy begins to feel her invisibility.

> Halfway into the silence for Norman Fisher, my arms were weightless.
> The rest came piecemeal as the moral started to compute.
> 1. The Rev Dogsbody had chosen this service to perform a miracle
> 2. He'd run time backwards, cleansed, absolved and got rid of the ground-in stain.
> 3. And the stain was me
> I didn't exist. The miracle had wiped me out. (Galloway 1994, 79)

The world is telling Joy that she does not exist, that she should blend into the background even more than the other women who simply submit to their man's wishes. In *The Bell Jar*, Sylvia Plath writes, 'I know that in spite of all the roses and kisses and restaurant dinners a man showered on a woman before he married her, what he secretly wanted when the wedding service ended was for her to flatten out underneath his feet like Mrs. Willard's kitchen mat' (Plath 1971, 69). Joy is not to simply flatten out. She is to disappear, to not exist. Joy is influenced by society. She cannot just disregard its wishes, and so, it is impossible for her to live, to act on her emotions, or to even have emotions without feeling an extraordinary sense of guilt for disturbing this non-existence which the world expects of her.

Scottish culture also puts pressure on Joy to repress her emotions, to keep them inside and out of sight. 'Love/Emotion = embarrassment: Scots equation. Exceptions are when roaring drunk or watching football. Men do rather better out of this loophole' (Galloway 1994, 82). Joy knows that her feelings are supposed to be hidden, and she tries to hold them in, but they cannot be controlled. They overwhelm her and she feels guilty, guilty for not being good' [where good = not putting anyone out by feeling too much, blank, unobtrusive]' (82). She is told that she is unwell and that this illness is the cause of her uncontrollable emotion. She is also told though, by doctors and friends, that she is to blame for her depression, for what is in her mind and invisible to all others. Dr Three says to Joy, 'You should ask to see me and now you're just wasting my time' (164). A Colleague from work says of the hospital, 'This. This place and everything. When I got the note from here. I'd never have figured. I thought you had more fight than that' (225). The people around Joy believe her problems can be solved simply with a little effort on her part just as Esther Greenwood's mother does when she says to her depressed daughter in *The Bell Jar*, 'I know you'd decide to be all right again' (Plath 1971, 119).

Joy, like many women suffering from depression, accepts the blame forced onto her. She believes her problems to be her own fault and pities those who waste their time dealing with her. 'Poor Dr Stead. I don't tell him the half of what I do. I'm a liar and a cheat with Dr Stead while he sees endless queues of sick people and tries to make room for me' (Galloway 1994, 95). Not feeling better after sessions with doctors and time in the hospital, Joy thinks to herself, 'Serves you right, you always expect too much' (165). As Elizabeth Wurtzel writes in her autobiographical *Prozac Nation*, 'I do feel sorry for all nice people whose efforts are wasted on a waste case like me. All this just amounts to more grist for the mill of the ill: On top of feeling sad, I also feel guilty' (Wurtzel 1994, 48).

In addition to her guilt for having feelings, for needing help, for being Michael's mistress, and for wasting 'real' people's time, Joy blames herself for not being perfect. She sees the beautiful and thin woman on magazine covers, reads the always flawless advice given inside for dealing with men, and scans the recipes for delicious muffins or breads listed in the back. She does not enjoy the way these images of perfection make her feel, yet she reads her magazines and watches the television day after day. 'I hate adverts. They are full of thin women doing exercises and smiling all the time. They make me feel guilty' (Galloway 1994, 37). She feels guilty and tries harder to be like them, to be what she feels is perfect, what her culture feels is perfect. Joy has nothing to do while she is 'lasting', and so she resorts to these impersonal forms of communication to which she does not have to give her feelings. She does not have to speak to the television or share her problems with it. This lack of communication that the media allows her to continue is one of the main barriers between depression and realisation for Joy. During a lecture in 1972, Anaïs Nin said, 'We cannot be aware of something in a non-language state. Our awareness somehow is connected with language. So it's very important at this point that women who have operated on a combination of instinct, emotion, intellect, and observation, a synthesis which we call intuition, somehow must learn to articulate, to become focused' (Nin 1975, 81). The television, like Joy's magazines, is simply a diversion from the chaos in her mind, but a diversion that only adds to her isolation and guilt. Joy's world has crumbled, and she feels it, feels it as if it came from her.

> I'm starting to hate things. I hate where I work. I see small things about too many small people and it makes me bitter. I don't want to be bitter. Bitterness hurts. I'm lonely. I'm afraid I'll go sour and nobody will love my any more. Something about me kills people. I'm losing days and drinking too much. I'm not a proper woman. I no longer menstruate. Sometimes I think I do not exist. I keep looking for the reasons and never find them, waiting all the time but I don't know what for. I always do the wrong thing (Galloway 1994, 105).

Self-destructive behaviour

Joy Stone presses pared lemons into her newly sliced fingers to feel the sting. She brushes her teeth until her gums bleed and the pit runs from her mouth a dark pink. She does not eat for days on end, and when she does, she swallows her hand to rid her light and empty body of any substance. She takes baths in steaming water that seems to burn off her skin. She cries after giving in to a man, after sex that she does not want. Joy inflicts pain on herself and allows others to do the same. There could be any number of psychological reasons for, or purposes of, this behaviour but several seem most consistent and in keeping with Joy's acts of self-mutilation: anorexia, bulimia, and alcoholism are acts of punishment, escape, control, and submission, as well as being cries for help. Her actions are the statements that she cannot make about the depression, grief, and guilt which have taken hold of her mind. Some of these purposes may seem to contradict each other, and they do. They work against each other and with each other in Joy's subconscious causing what are always acts of violence. The physical pain Joy feels proves her existence while bringing her closer to death, closer to non-existence. While preparing to commit suicide, Joy realises, 'I don't want to live very much but I don't want to die' (203). This paradox parallels the one relating to a woman's guilt. Women want to realise their potential, but they do not want to disturb or bother anyone around them. So Joy is caught, caught between submission and control, between punishment and escape, caught as these women are between taking action and the guilt that comes with it. She is trapped on her island and crying for help with only pills and knives and an urge to hurt herself.

Joy blames herself for the problems in her life, for Michael's death and her reaction to it. She slices the insides of her arms, burns her fingers, and draws blood when brushing her teeth in order to punish herself. She blames herself for bingeing on chocolate biscuits after two young and beautiful senior girls some to visit her. She throws up within a quarter of an hour as a punishment. The guilt in her mind is transferred into physical action. Causing herself physical pain is supposed to make Joy feel less guilt, though of course that is not the outcome. 'I leaned over the sink and brushed my teeth hard till the spit went dark pink, pressing the brush into the gum to punish myself enough so god would let Myra leave me alone' (59). The pain does not really ease the tumultuous swirl of pain and guilt and sadness in her mind. It only becomes more regular, more comfortable, and more of a routine.

> … Then I will go home and wash my hair, scrape away the hospital and the punters' smoke, brush my teeth till the gums bleed
> Then

> I like routines. You can get cosy in a rut. You can pretend things are the same when they're not. Knowing I need to live with lies makes me more anxious, depressed and guilty. This way I need routines more (156).

Joy is comfortable with the pain she causes herself. She barely notices it. It gives her life a sense of normalcy, a sense of regularity that is calming in its juxtaposition to the chaos that she really feels. The actual bleeding fingers and acidic taste in the mouth give Joy a momentary escape from her mind as well. To combat the constant press of guilt and grief, she generates physical pain that preoccupies her thoughts, allowing them a brief repose from her genuine feelings. Roy Baumeister writes in *Escaping the Self* (1991, 167) that binge eaters like Joy are unpleasantly self-conscious people who practice unusual restraint in eating when attention is on them, but who binge when alone in order to escape from this self-consciousness which so controls their lives. He also writes, 'Bulimics in general seem to have attitudes about time similar to those of suicidal persons. The future looks bleak, full of further misfortunes and disasters, and the past is clouded with catastrophes and problems that cannot be overcome. The only solace is to escape into a narrowly defined present' (169). Joy escapes into this present from the too-high standards that she reads about in magazines, from her guilt, and from the thought of having to actually face her real problems.

People do exhibit a variety of patterns of self-defeating behaviour. They sabotage their own performances, endanger their health and well-being, undermine their material goals, and even condemn themselves to emotionally painful circumstances. There is no evidence that people *desire* these unpleasant outcomes, but they do choose them when the alternative is an acutely painful awareness of self. When a person's image of self is at stake, [it is a way] of avoiding unwelcome thoughts of the self as incompetent, unworthy, unlovable unattractive, or otherwise deficient (44–5).

Mary Piper writes (1995, 174) that an anorexic woman's message to the world around her is 'You can't make me eat more. I am in control of my fate, even if my fate is starving'. Joy says just this in her attempt to control her life by controlling her intake of food. Her emotions and her life are pure chaos, but the food that enters Joy's body is restricted and highly organised. It is her means of feigning control, control which she knows does not really exist but tries nonetheless to keep up. She displays this also in purging, showing that even if a substance enters her body, she can remove it, grab it out of her insides and fling it from her in order to preserve her cleanliness, her willpower and restraint. Joy can even get rid of a man. 'He kissed me again before he went for the car and I came in and threw up like an animal' (Galloway 1994, 100). It is her talent, her calling (just as Sylvia Plath's calling in the poem 'Lady Lazarus' was to die exceptionally well), her strength. She has power over her body, power to scar it or to starve it, and she abuses this power because it is the only way she can make herself feel strong. 'In bed, I run my hands over the reclaimed ribs, the bony shoulders like wingsprouts. I balance the gin on the rug and feel the flat bowl of my hips. They're sharp on either side for the first time I remember. Like a man's. Laughter shakes the mattress. I laugh till the neighbours thump on the wall' (90). There is pride in that laughter, pride and an imagined sense of control.

In the last stanza of 'Cut', Sylvia Plath finally admits her self-hatred and acknowledges her role as a '"dirty girl" with something missing to make her pure and whole' (Bundtzen 1983, 248).

> How you jump—
> Trepanned veteran,
> Dirty girl,
> Thumb stump.

The act of slicing off the top of her thumb is seen as submissive and passive. She has acted, but acted in accordance with her self-destructive impulses and given up control. Joy does the same, acting in submission, doing to herself what society has already done and continues to do. She gives up and sleeps with Tony after subtle protests that he either fails to see or chooses to ignore. 'I gave in... He couldn't find a way inside my dress. I undid the buttons myself to make it quicker' (Galloway 1994, 175). Joy admits that the guilt is stronger than she is, and so starves herself as the magazines say to do, sleeps with men who want it as society says it is a woman's place to do, and represses her emotions as Scottish culture says it is most appropriate to do. She becomes small, taking the place that she has been told to take.

> Anorexia is a metaphor. It is a young woman's statement that she will become what the culture asks of its women, which is that they be thin and non-threatening. Anorexia signifies that a young woman is so delicate that, like the women of China with their tiny broken feet, she needs a man to shelter and protect her from a world she cannot handle. Anorexic women signal with their bodies 'I will take up only a small amount of space. I won't get in the way.' They signal 'I won't be intimidating or threatening.' (Who is afraid of a seventy-pound adult?) (Piper 1995, 175)

Joy's actions convey a surrender, a surrender to the emotions that run her mind and to the society which runs her life. She is treated as if she does not exist, and so she says: 'I toy with suicide. I toy with pills,... with broken glass and razor blades, juggernauts and tops of tall stairwells' (Galloway 1994, 199). She toys with non-existence, with absolute compliance with the powers in her life. She toys with killing herself, with becoming the non-existent woman that people see in her.

Lastly, Joy's actions are a cry for attention, for help. She is showing her insides through the scars and burns on her arms. She slices open her knuckles and blood oozes out. Her insides ooze out. Joy says that she has 'a layer of missing skin' (143), but really she is just full of holes, small burn holes and long slits of opened flesh. She is aware of what it is that lies under her scarred skin, but she also knows the trick is to keep it hidden. 'I shove unidentifiable debris under the rug and hope it stays put. Superficially everything looks fine but underneath is another story. I never wash out the bin or scour the sink. The grease beneath the cooker turns my stomach but doesn't stop me sweeping more under there: dried up breadcrumbs and frozen peas, flakes of onion skin' (92). Joy knows the trick to keep hidden debris from view, though. 'The trick,' she says, 'is not to look,' (92) but her skin is thin and dry like tissue paper and so full of holes that the underside, the inside of her is there for all to see. In fact, she has made her skin that way so that someone can see, someone who will finally look, someone like herself.

About the grief and guilt that have pervaded her entire body, Joy says, 'There was an undertone of sex to all this but only by association: depression isn't sexy' (132). Elizabeth Wurtzel conveys the same message in writing about the death and life of Sylvia Plath.

> Forget about the scant hours in her brief life when Sylvia Plath was able to produce the works in *Ariel*. Forget about that tiny bit of time and just remember the days that spanned into years when she could not move, couldn't think straight, could only lie in wait in a hospital bed, hoping for the relief that electroconvulsive therapy would bring. Don't think of the striking on-screen picture, the mental movie you create of the pretty young woman being wheeled on the gurney to get her shock treatments, and don't think of the psychedelic, photonegative image of this same woman at the moment she receives that bolt of electricity. Think, instead, of the girl herself, of the way she must have felt right then, of the way no amount of great poetry and fascination and fame could make the pain she felt at that moment worth suffering. Remember that when you're at the point at which you're doing something as desperate and violent as sticking your head in an oven, it is only because the life that proceeded this act felt even worse. (Wurtzel 1994, 295–6).

Joy's violent acts and dreams of suicide are not romantic or sexy. They are the physical embodiment of her feelings. Life seems pointless to Joy. Living seems pointless. She only commits these violent and desperate acts because her life feels so much worse than they do, than carving into the 'fishbelly white' of her arm does. She cannot attack the thoughts in her mind, so her body endures the pain. 'I want to unpick pieces from my head and not feel like this. You can't get away from the inside of your own head. Look, I am not a bad woman. I have committed no act of malice. But everything I touch turns bad. Christmas is coming and I have nothing to give... It gets worse every day' (Galloway 1994, 177). Joe does not understand. She does not see why she is depressed. She only sees it as something in her, something she has caused. So on top of feeling sad, she feels guilty, and this guilt is for more than just being sad. It is for being alive, for being who she is, a Scottish woman alone on her own island, unable to swim and unable to forgive herself.

In the end, Joy does begin to forgive herself. She does begin to let go of the guilt, and she screams, releasing anger and grief and blame in a way that causes her no physical harm. Acid burns and bleeding knuckles will no longer be needed as Joy has found her voice and found a way around her calling for physical pain.

Works cited

Baumeister, Roy F. (1991) *Escaping the Self: Alcoholism, Spirituality, Masochism and Other Flights from the Burden of Selfhood*. New York: Basic Books.

Bundtzen, Lynda K. (1983) *Plath's Incarnations: Woman and the Creative Process*. Ann Arbor: University of Michigan Press.

Galloway, Janice (1991) 'Introduction', *Meantime: Looking Forward to the New Millennium*. Janice Galloway (Ed.). Edinburgh: Polygon.

Galloway, Janice (1994) *The Trick is to Keep Breathing*. Normal, Illinois: Dalkey Archive Press.

Piper, Mary (1995) *Reviving Ophelia: Saving the Selves of Adolescent Girls*. New York: Ballantine Books.

Plath, Sylvia (1971) *The Bell Jar*. New York: Harper & Row, Publishers.

Plath, Sylvia (1961) 'Cut', *Ariel*. New York: Harper & Row, Publishers.

Nin, Anaïs (1975) *A Woman Speaks: The Lectures, Seminars, and Interviews of Anaïs Nin*. Evelyn J. Hinz (Ed.). Athens, Ohio: Swallow Press.

Wurtzel, Elizabeth (1994) *Prozac Nation*. New York: Riverhead Books.

Children of a larger growth?

The men in Janice Galloway's short fiction

Colin Clark

In a previous incarnation as a high school English teacher I was asked to supervise a science class, third-year foundation level, about a dozen boys. I was fair game and they knew it. I arrived in the classroom, feigning confidence, took the register, and got the boys started on the work that had been left for them. Then I prayed for peace. For ten minutes the boys seemed to be doing their work; at the end of those ten minutes things started to unravel.

'Sir, what team do you support?'

'Shh. On with your work.'

'No, really, Sir. What team?'

'Never mind. You should be working.'

You can't ignore them—not for long—you can't distract them, and the threat of sanctions will either provoke derisive laughter or encourage them to push their luck to the limit. So I replied:

'No team. I'm not interested in football.'

'Aye, right. Is it Celtic or Rangers?'

'I'll tell you after class.'

'Did you see the game last night?'

'What game?'

Silence. Then . . .

'Sir, you married?'

'Nope.'

Some muttering. Not married. Doesn't like football. In the twisted logic of the school playground, the syllogism is completed . . .

'Backs to the wall, lads. The teacher's a poof.'

I should have lied.

The aim of this essay is to provide a reading of Janice Galloway's short fiction from a male perspective. I hadn't been a male reader before. I have been a reader, certainly, a male all my life, but I had never put the two together, never considered being male as having anything to do with the activity of reading. 'Maleness' was something I hadn't thought about much, a bit like being right-handed, or brown-eyed. The only times I have questioned what it is to be male are when I have come across occasional bizarre generalisations, usually around the subject of football. In Scotland, *all* men like football.

Reading Galloway's work, her interviews, and criticism about her work, I realise that not having to think about your gender as a reader is a somewhat privileged position that we men have occupied for quite a while. We don't even have to think about it. The male point of view has dominated literature, ruled all our reading habits. Writing, for long enough, *was* the male point of view—for some it still is, particularly in relation to the construction of literary canons that dictate what gets taught in universities. As Galloway herself has observed, to be a Scottish writer was to be a man: Scottish writing was men writing.

Teaching English in secondary schools you are at the mercy of many things, among them the availability of resources in the department, or what's in the book cupboard. It's interesting to look at the two most common school anthologies of Scottish writing (at least in the schools I have worked in) to see how much things have changed. One is *Identities*, published in 1981, reprinted several times, now probably out of print. A quick inventory of its contents reveals that of twenty-nine writers, four (or 14%) are women (Catherine Lucy Czerkawska, Liz Lochhead, Janet Sandison and Molly Weir.) This anthology predates those writers we are now familiar with such as Jackie Kay, Janet Paisley, Ali Smith, Margaret Elphinstone, A.L. Kennedy, Louise Welsh, and of course Janice Galloway. A later anthology for schools, *Shouting It Out*, published in 1995, redressed this imbalance: of the ten writers represented, six (or 60%) are women, among them Galloway, Kennedy, Paisley and Lochhead. Tom Pow's introduction to this latter anthology mentions the 'moment of realisation of change or the desire for change' that many of the writers deal with in their contributions, and the anthology as a whole addresses that desire in relation to the experiences and representations that Scottish school children in 1995 had of their own culture in literature. The focus of Pow's introduction is not on women's writing, but his selection of contributors might well have been. Who had realised in 1981 there was a need or even a desire for change in the gender imbalance in Scottish literature? Plenty of people, plenty of readers, even a few men no doubt, but where were they?

Back to school. There exist some popularly held myths about what it is to be male, and in my experience high schools provide the strongest and most extreme assertions of masculinity—many of them negative. Perhaps it's understandable. Schools are a crucible of the emotions: enclosed, restricted environments containing the hormonal reactions going on inside teenagers. It is a place where identities are forged. School is where we learn all kinds of things, some useful, some malign. It's where some people learn to bully and others learn to perceive themselves as worthless; it's where lifelong habits like smoking and drinking are learned from persuasive peers; it's where anger is allowed to spill, often unchecked and unrestrained, into violence. It's where our sexual orientations are challenged and interrogated; where any slight deviation from a narrowly defined consensus is perceived as evidence of homosexuality; where differences of any kind are persecuted mercilessly with racism, misogyny, homophobia. Sticks and stones. Dangerous behaviours are grown and nurtured in schools like bacteria in a Science lab Petri dish.

I was to come across the familiar language of the playground a lot in Janice Galloway's short stories, usually in the mouths of males, and I started off wondering whether her male characters were anything other than over-grown adolescents, or as John Dryden put it, 'children of a larger growth'. The language of Galloway's male characters tends to be colloquial, often bad-tempered, frequently abusive:

'GIRLS ARE A BUNCH OF CUNTS' ('Blood', *Blood*, p. 5)

BASTARDS! SPIKY HEIDED BASTARDS. AD GIE THEM PUNK. WHAT DO THEY THINK THEY LOOK LIKE EH? JUST WHAT DO THEY THINK THEYRE AT EH! ('Scenes from the Life No.23: Parental Advice', *Blood*, p. 12)

Their behaviour isn't much better:

> The dark man stopped, his fist raised. He looked round.
>> Somebody's supposed to get hurt, that's the fuckin idea. ('Need for Restraint', *Blood*, p. 83)

And in the end, though men may hurt each other, it's usually a woman who gets it worst.

> …some body was dragging me by the neck a man he said YOU'RE COMING WITH ME but his voice wasn't right like he was choking or crying maybe something was wrong it was definitely the man saying YOU'RE COMING WITH ME and he shoved one of his hands up under my jersey I could feel the big shape of his hand sort of pulling my jersey under my jacket and going up onto my belly and it made me stop and breathe wrong… ('Last Thing', *Where You Find It*, pp. 176–7)

Or in this instance, a girl:

> And I hit her NOT hard to begin with but she just LOOKS not even FLINCHING when you TOLD her what would happen so I did it again STAND UP KIMBERLEY curling in a corner NOT EVEN TRYING TO STAND UP just watching while I shook her, I lifted her up put the cigarette against the skin of the wrist IT WAS MEANT TO BE A LESSON . . . ('Someone Had To', *Where You Find It*, p. 124)

The title of this story reads like a grown-up version of the typical schoolboy excuse when accused of some misdemeanour, *it wisny me*. It suggests a lack of culpability, freedom from blame. Men are above the law because men *are* the law:

> Well, he said. His voice was louder than it had been. Where do we go from here, young lady?
>> Alice kept her head down.
> ('A Proper Respect', *Where You Find It*, p. 134)

The patronising doctor in 'A Proper Respect' is trying to educate Alice in the error of her ways, using his authority to force the girl into making a number of decisions she has no control over. This is a world where a girl can have a child and sign for its treatment, but is allowed no say over what happens to her own body—it has to be a man's world. The 'respect' of the title is ironic. We can no longer operate within the old hierarchies, where respect is automatically conferred on men in positions of power. Like doctors, teachers, even parents:

SAMMY: Show your daddy youre no feart son. I'll catch you. Dont be feart, this is your da talkin to you. Come on. For me. Jump and I'll catch you. Don't be scared. Sammy, son, I'm waiting. I'm ready.

A few more seconds of tense silence click out of the clock. WEE SAMMY *blinks. His hands lift from the wall and he decides: one breath and he throws himself from the screaming height of the sill. In the same second,* SAMMY *skirts to the side. The boy crashes lumpily into the tiles of the fire surround. His father sighs and averts his eyes, choking back a sob.*

SAMMY: 'Let that be a lesson to you, son. Trust nae cunt.'
           ('Scenes From the Life No.23: Parental Advice', *Blood*, p.16)

The lessons men teach in Galloway's fiction are brutal ones. Is this a masculine idea of how the world works? Or is it the way it really is? I remember similar advice from my grandfather—without the vertigo—advising me to open up to no-one, to play my cards close to my chest, not to let anybody know my business. He was a Glasgow East Ender, a bit of a hard man in his day, I came to learn, and he wasn't unaccustomed to doling out some tough love of his own. Through his actions, his words, his love for me and my family, he also taught me about unconditional positive regard, respect, familial love. Lots of useful things, positive things, that Galloway's poor men seem never to have encountered.

Trust nae cunt. There is something flinty hard, bitter, maybe even old-fashioned about the sentiment, though there is nothing old-fashioned about the use of the word 'cunt'. Although the word has existed in our language for centuries, its use and abuse has made for some heated discussion and it remains one of the most controversial and offensive words in English (except in some parts of urban Scotland where it is perversely considered a term of affection among men). In 'Blood', however, the people—we assume they are boys—who write this phrase (with accompanying crude pictures) as a graffito on the door to the girls' toilets clearly intend to offend. Not only do they succeed in that, they also manage to cause the girls to avoid using the toilet if at all possible. Sexual territory aggressively demarcated. The language of the playground, violent and misogynist. The ideology of difference. If language is power, then in this story it is in the hands of the boys; theirs is the power to silence, to name and even to claim private female-only spaces as their own. Far from reclaiming the word 'cunt', as some feminists have sought to, Galloway alerts us that this kind of language is firmly in the linguistic territorial domain of men.

> . . . he turns and he's oot wi this stick christ big fuckin cue right WOOF roon his heid like a WOOF fuckin caber or somethin nearly RIGHT IN THE EYE I says WOOF fuckin COOL IT jist WOOF lassie screamin he's taken his tee-shirt this TAP fuckin tap aff this sweat like a hoor an this TAP aff . . .' ('Scenes from the Life No. 29: Dianne', *Blood,* p.31)

At the end of 'Dianne', we are told the woman who observes this conversation taking place below her window 'goes on looking down' on these men. The repetition in the final two lines: 'But only at you. Only at you.' suggests an attitude of condescension from the writer, as well as the literal point of view of the woman at the window. The standard English voice and orthography of the narration contrast strikingly with the non-standard representation of the men's speech—full of block capitals, swear words and irregular punctuation—and makes their language stand out as abrasive and uneducated. In Galloway's short stories block capitals are used frequently to represent male speech. It seems like the men are always shouting, angry and, in comparison to the crafted language of the narration, unsubtle.

In 'Valentine', the husband's lack of interest in language or his inability to use words creatively is tied up with his refusal to express emotion. In this case his love for his wife, if he has any, is expressed materially; a thing, a card with someone else's words on it is proxy for his emotions. If the graffiti on the girls' toilet door in 'Blood' represents male ownership of language and territory, here we have a very different view of male relationships with language, with emotion, and with women: put them together and men become inarticulate, dumb:

> Despite me, the card is always there on the table when I get up, a boxful of something padded with hearts on the front and a poem that I scour

with my eyes trying to get below the surface and feel what it was that made him choose this one, which parts of it are closest to what he would say to himself if he ever said things like that out loud. Only he doesn't. People don't, he says. That's what you buy the cards for. ('Valentine', *Where You Find It*, p. 1)

If men are strangers to women, at times their speech is like a foreign language:

KETL
A word and a sound like a tearing sheet make me turn abruptly.
KETLHEN IH
The fat man crammed the living-room doorway. I had heard nothing of his approach and here he was right inside the room, speaking. He sipped self-consciously from an invisible cup to help me with the words.
KETTLE. ONY TEA. ('Plastering the Cracks', *Blood*, p. 94)

Men speak a different language from women, that's the assumption. Male speech can be a bit comical, a bit angry, a bit rude. And in Galloway's fiction, it possesses none of the craft and sophistication that we get in the narrative passages.

Perhaps this is fair enough. The language is not unfamiliar; we've all heard it. The kinds of words used across urban Scotland in daily discourse *are* offensive to women. Women have lacked a prominent literary voice that speaks for their reality, and consequently we men are unaccustomed to having our speech represented by women—this is what we sound like to a woman's ear. And it's not that pleasant.

But I wonder if Galloway sows the seeds of her own undoing. The problem for me is that by representing male speech as orthographically non-standard in such an extreme manner, the men come over as caricatures, two-dimensional cartoons, and not real men. Certainly, the volume level on the man-speak in *Where You Find It* has been turned down a notch or two: there are fewer block capitals, fewer instances of blank unintelligibity, fewer outbursts of rage. The characters are also more subtle, more filled out, even if the view of male behaviour is as uncompromisingly critical. But in *Blood*, while I'm swept off my feet by the skill and the musicality of Galloway's prose, I hear bum notes in the male chorus.

In 'Uncle Felix' one of the female characters says of men:

'They're all the same, football and fighting and drink. Motorcars. Wee boys. Bloody men'. (*Blood*, p. 172)

Bloody men. Warmongers. Abusers. Harbingers of blood. Maybe we are, but it's not all we are: the prose may sing in glorious polyphony but this restricted, bleak view of men in Galloway's short fiction often sounds like a tune with one note.

I would like to conclude by returning to school, and to the title story from *Blood*, and think about music a little bit more.

The story is set mostly in a school and concerns an unnamed female pupil. She encounters various kinds of men during and after a visit to the dentist whom we first meet with his knee up on the girl's chest, wielding a pair of pliers in order to gain greater purchase on a tooth he is attempting to extract. At the other end of the story, once the girl has returned to school and the 'fresh and clean' rehearsal room with the rosewood piano and Mozart, the girl's music teacher Mr Gregg pops into the narration to tell us that the male student teacher who is rehearsing next door 'is afraid of the girls and who can blame him ha ha.' The girl doesn't '[understand] the joke too well', and to be honest, neither do I. Is the student teacher genuinely afraid of girls? Why would that be? Was he bullied by them? Maybe he's just shy. On the other hand, teaching, working with young people, can be a dangerous job, more so now than it ever was—one of the first pieces of professional advice I received from a (female) colleague was never to let myself be alone in a room with a female student. Perhaps someone has given the student teacher similar advice and this is why he flees the room once the girl begins to bleed from the mouth. No telling what people might assume, what suspicions might fall.

'Blood' is often interpreted as being about male theft of language from the mouths of women. True, the girl, the main character, is unable to speak at all: the power of language has been extracted (temporarily) by the dentist along with her tooth leaving her powerless to respond when the student teacher comes in.

I think it is interesting, though, that what the girl does have is music, or rather the ability to communicate *through* music. Music restores to the girl's world some semblance of control, since she seems previously to have lost control over her own body, particularly her blood. I don't think it matters that the piece she is playing was written by a male composer, the point is that she makes it her own: her interpretation of the music is what causes the student teacher to hear, to listen, to forget his fear of girls. Ultimately the music moves him to speak to her, to express his appreciation of her playing. The dentist may have stolen the words from her mouth and the boys vandalised the girls' toilets with abusive slogans, but music is a deeper emotional language that the girl is able to communicate with, and it bonds her—albeit temporarily and abortively—to another human being.

Maybe it's wishful thinking, maybe I'm plain wrong, but it seems to me that Janice Galloway doesn't so much write about the differences between men and women as dig about in the roots of all human behaviour, the really interesting bits where the worlds of men and women collide. That there are differences is unquestionable, but they are rather like the girl's extracted tooth: a little twisted at the root, but in the end everything comes down to the red stuff. Blood, and music—It's what we share.

Works cited

Galloway, Janice (1992) *Blood*. London: Minerva. [1991]
—— (1997) *Where You Find It*. London: Vintage. [1996]
Pow, Tom (Ed.) (1998) *Shouting It Out*. London: Hodder & Stoughton. [1995]
Thomson, Gilles (Ed.) (1990) *Identities*. London: Heinemann. [1981]

Looking as though you're in control

Janice Galloway and the working-class female gothic

Alexis Logsdon

'Poltergeist. I thought the hair bristling on my neck was just from the house settling in and from watching the movie: horror pictures affect me that way.'—Joy Stone (in Galloway 1991b, 129).

'[A]ll you have to do is follow some people around and look at their existence for 24 hours, and it will be horror. It will just be horror.'—James Kelman (in Punter 1999, 103).

The gothic novel has had many turns since its invention nearly three hundred years ago. By the time Mary Shelley wrote *Frankenstein*, the form had already undergone extensive reinvention and revision. In the second half of the twentieth century, writers such as Flannery O'Connor, Muriel Spark, Angela Carter, and Margaret Atwood have created a new gothic novel recharged by feminist—or at least woman-centred—ideologies. These authors represent the female body and its functions most often deemed unpleasant as a force to be reckoned with or an enemy unto itself, to varied results.

Like the work of many of her contemporaries, much of Janice Galloway's fiction focuses on the perils of (and to) the female body. In this sense Galloway borrows from the gothic, but her fictional world is not limited to this genre. While Galloway addresses many of the concerns of gothic women writers in regard to gender, and particularly female identity, she also challenges the form in order to discuss how class and social position operate in women's oppression. Further, an exploration of the gothic through Galloway can expand our definition of this genre as well. I propose to explore the ways in which a gothic reading of Galloway can both enhance and limit understanding of her fiction. Galloway's fiction will be read through a gothic lens, foregrounding a socio-political reading over the psychoanalytic reading most often applied to the gothic novel.

Feminist critics have long been concerned with gothic fiction. The imperilled heroines; foregrounding of women's place in the family and society; a focus on female gender construction and the dangers of its enforcement; and resistance to these constrictions on women—all interests of the gothic novel—make it particularly attractive to feminists. Michelle Massé (1992) claims that resistance takes three forms in the gothic novel: 'aggression against the dominator...; self-conscious subversion that mimes cultural expectations of femininity to achieve the protagonist's freedom; and a utopian alterity that refuses to accept the binary options of subordinated/oppressed and laughs heartily at the very idea' (240). Massé adds that the last of these forms of resistance is for the future, 'only hinted at because still unrealised' (240). But it is this last form that is most present in Galloway's novels. Both typographically and thematically Galloway attempts to break free from narrative conventions, but her focus is on the gendered, class-specific threats to 'the protagonist's freedom.' While this focus in Galloway's work need not be read as explicitly gothic, the term is useful when looked at in conjunction with other aspects of Galloway's fiction.

While some critics have pointed to a gothic sensibility in much recent Scottish fiction, few have examined the implications of this. Recent anthologies *Damage Land: New Scottish Gothic Fiction* and *The New Gothic*, numerous comparisons of Galloway to other authors deemed gothic, and criticism under the gothic rubric all point to Galloway as a gothic writer. David Punter identifies several gothic features in Galloway's writing: *The Trick is to Keep Breathing* is an 'account of a consciousness forced apart' (Punter 1999, 104); 'asylums are Gothic' (109); and themes of 'disastrous families, ...sexual hatred, ...[and an] inability to see the surroundings without an in-built mechanism of distortion' are evocative of both 'the older and the modern Scottish Gothic' (112). Engaged with recent gothic criticism, Punter focuses on psychological themes in Galloway, but rarely expands his reading to fully question the socio-political dimensions of Joy Stone's need for an 'in-built mechanism of distortion' (112) to survive, opting instead to view the 'forced apart' (104) consciousness primarily as a conflict of nationality instead of gender or class. Punter points provocatively to a connection between gothic elements in recent Scottish literature and 'long-suppressed narrative[s] of abuse' (112) but does not look at implications beyond his interpretation of the repressed emotional nature of this fiction. Christie Leigh March remarks, 'Galloway's use of the fantastic also extends to the macabre...illustrating larger social problems through her conflation of unruly bodies and threatening landscapes' (126–7). March goes further to look at Joy's social conditions; though she does not describe Galloway's work as gothic, March sees in her most gothic elements a commentary on the heroines' social conditions. The class-specific peril Galloway's heroines suffer suggests a gothic world beyond the psychological realm focused on in much gothic criticism.

The contested castle and changing landscapes

Galloway's first novel, *The Trick is to Keep Breathing*, recalls the nervous breakdown of Joy Stone, a drama teacher and part-time bookie's office cashier whose lover, Michael, drowns while they are on vacation. The novel plots the traumatic aftermath of Michael's death, when Joy is nearly evicted from the flat she and Michael shared, and is denied the right to mourn because she is technically Michael's mistress. Joy voluntarily enters a psychiatric hospital after at least two failed suicide attempts. Galloway includes play script, graphics, and non-standard typesetting to cobble together a collage of Joy's troubled life. The novel simultaneously explores Joy's emotional, corporal and geographic terrains: the homes Joy inhabits, her connection with her own and other people's bodies, and the typography of the novel work together to illustrate Joy's devastated state. Whether her homes are threatened by structural damage or state intervention, they point to Joy's instability due to her precarious class position.

Galloway's treatment of unstable homes evokes the gothic trope of the disintegrating home. According to Kate Ferguson Ellis, eighteenth- and nineteenth-century gothic novels discuss the home by 'focusing on crumbling castles as sites of terror, and on homeless protagonists who wander the face of the earth,' but 'it is the failed home that appears on [the earlier gothic novels'] pages, the place from which some... are locked out, and others... are locked in' (ix). In Galloway's work, too, home is a recurring problem. In *The Trick is to Keep Breathing*, Joy wanders from her mother's hostile home to her own seemingly peaceful, yet secretly rotting, cottage to the council house she shares with Michael. Even the home of her best friend's mother, Ellen, with its trappings of middle-class, material comfort, feels awkward to Joy. Though the reasons for her unease in each home differ, one thing binds them: Joy is unable to feel truly at home anywhere because she cannot conform to society's standards. Too poor to afford a better cottage, Joy must accept her disintegrating home; her home with Michael is not really hers because they are not married; and the mental hospital, though it serves a purpose, can never be a permanent home. Joy dwells in the 'urban and domestic landscapes Galloway creates' which 'underlie the daily injustices [she] suffer[s]' (March 128), and reflect her status as a single, working-class woman. Joy returns to work soon after Michael's death, before she is ready:

Tuesday Morning
I have to go to work.
I have to go to work because
      1. it will be warmer than here;
      2. it brings home the bacon;
      3. there will be people.

I wrap up in two layers of clothes against the frost (Galloway 1991b, 70).

Here Joy not only inhabits the 'urban and domestic landscapes Galloway creates' (March 2003, 128), but a typographical landscape as well. The non-standard punctuation suggests Joy's unreadiness to return to work, highlighting as it does her incoherent, depressed state. At the same time, the numbered list of somewhat tongue-in-cheek reasons she must go back to work is an indictment of a system that would require her to return to work to 'bring home the bacon' (Galloway 1991b, 70) so soon after her lover's death. The businesslike, logical structure of the list becomes preposterous in the context of Galloway's typography; the list appears on a page that Galloway chose not to number, further polarizing the logic of the world of work and Joy's emotional state. The list also serves to point out Joy's isolation within her community and the substandard conditions in which she lives: though she has neighbours, Joy must go to work to be around people; additionally, her home is too poorly heated to keep her warm, either because she cannot afford heat or because the building is poorly insulated and provides her

148

another reason to go to work. Thus Galloway weaves the setting, the typography, and Joy's emotional landscape together to bring to light the hard realities of working life for contemporary women, creating a new gothic heroine concerned with both the haunting and emotional instability of the traditional gothic, and the material reality of working-class life.

It is in her mother's home that Joy learns to keep up appearances: 'I looked down my nose at the windolene sheen of my mother's house and knew better while my mother revved the hoover in the background and told me I was a lazy bitch' (18). This is Joy's earliest experience of class-consciousness in the home. Significantly, she defies her mother, vowing to eschew pretensions of class. Ironically, she later must keep up these appearances herself to ward off the housing official and the health visitor.

Initially, Joy's cottage seems a refuge. It is her first home on her own (she has recently broken up with a man she had dated since high school) and she enjoys the freedom of her own space. This is soon shattered, however, when Michael moves into the cottage and discovers a fungus in the kitchen that turns out to be dry rot, a scourge that will eventually eat the house from the inside out. What 'at first looks like a refuge from the grimness of urban decay' becomes an 'appalling architecture…not so easily evaded [that] leaves its own bloody traces on the disintegrating mind' (Punter 1999, 107). In other words, this false refuge is a metonymic emblem of Joy's sense of security, a symbol of her unstable position both as a woman and as an underpaid schoolteacher. While the cottage represents the fragile state of Joy and Michael's relationship, it also serves as a mirage for Joy as a working-class woman: Joy moves into the cottage because of its suspiciously low cost, but is not able to afford the repairs the house requires. March (2003, 116) observes that for Joy, 'the domestic environment itself ceases to be a woman's domain and becomes hostile'. However, the home here does not become hostile to Joy specifically as a woman, but to Joy and Michael as a couple whose relationship does not fit easily into legal boundaries and therefore must be punished. Here Galloway explores the ambiguity of gender roles as a marker of subjugation. Both men and women suffer when the home is threatened. Though the nature and degree of their suffering varies, both Michael and Joy are imperilled when the stability of their home is threatened. Whereas in an earlier tradition of the gothic novel the home is portrayed as the site of inherently female displacement, men in Galloway's work are adversely affected by the unstable home as well.

This punishment does not end when they leave the cottage and move into council housing that is only intended for Michael. When Michael dies in

Spain, Joy's domestic comfort is once again threatened, this time more explicitly by the state. Joy is required to beg to stay in the house, and is forcibly reminded of her status as interloper by the housing authority representative, Mr Dick. The anxiety enforced upon Joy is evident as she prepares for Mr Dick's visit, and is deepened by what he has to tell her:

> I clean the kitchen till my hands are swollen from cold water, red as ham. My knuckles scrape and go lilac till the kitchen looks like they do on TV and smells of synthetic lemons and wax...I try not to worry. I try to be grateful since it took me long enough to get here, haggling with tiny-minded Mr Dick from the Housing Authority. Every fourth house in this estate is empty...But Mr Dick said there were difficulties in my getting tenancy...There were rent arrears...I said I hadn't got the money.
>
> Mr Dick looked me right in the eye.
>   Try to be a little more cooperative...Strictly speaking, we're under no obligation to house you at all, not when you were never registered as a tenant...
> I said I was sorry about all the trouble they were having on my account... But I didn't have any money. (Galloway 1991b, 18).

In the mode of Kafka and James Kelman, Galloway presents the bureaucratic state as impossibly cold and impersonal. As with the health visitor and the nameless psychiatrists Joy visits, Mr Dick is unsympathetic and impenetrable. Galloway highlights the unwarranted entry of the state into Joy's life with the housing worker's name: Mr Dick, a vulgar, even violent term for the penis. Though Mr Dick is impenetrable, he, and by extension the state, penetrates Joy's home. Although there is no shortage of housing at the council estate, Joy's continued tenancy is threatened by the state. In contrast to the 'fortress'-like eighteenth century gothic home (Ellis 1989, xi), the gothic home of Galloway is the site of constant invasion.

When Joy is institutionalised, she becomes even further alienated from a sense of home. Karen F. Stein (1983, 126) observes that madness in gothic heroines often serves as a 'critique of the society which has prevented her from developing her full human potential'. Further, the manner in which society treats the mentally ill often indicates how these people are judged by that society; Joy is reduced to a child, offered no privacy, and inundated with the smells of the unwell: 'The ward smells funny,' and 'the pyjamas look bloody awful. Tesco's: girls' aged 11. Terrible.' (Galloway 1991b, 137) The ward attendant 'broadcasts my hiding place in the end room, and [the group therapy leader] Tom announces my job as a joke' (145). Yet even as Joy lives in fear of this new 'home' as much as her council flat, she is equally if not more afraid of wandering outdoors. Galloway presents Joy's world as marked by dark, dangerous spaces. During a weekend away from the institution, Joy contemplates her return:

> This time tomorrow I'll be back in Foresthouse. I don't want to be there either. I walk across the moorland between town and the Boot Hill towers listening for the noises in the dark. All sorts of lunatics hang around the estate waiting for what turns up…I keep walking up the middle of the road, following advice from a magazine about how not to get raped…Looking as though you're in control. (130)

The journey from one 'home' to another is as frightening for Joy as inhabiting either of them. Because her home is far from the centre of town Joy is forced to traverse isolated fields to get there. The psychiatric hospital's name, Foresthouse, itself signifies a fear of both indoor and outdoor space. Despite the fairytale name, the hospital is not the 'crumbling castle' (Ellis 1989, ix) of early gothic fiction. What initially sounds like a pastoral haven proves to be no safer than anywhere else. Thus Galloway highlights the impossibility of safety and freedom for a woman of Joy's social class.

Unlike traditional gothic protagonists, the women in Galloway's fiction are not bourgeois women trapped by society and social mores in their fathers' homes. Instead, Galloway's menacing homes are signifiers of working- and lower-middle-class instability, and more explicitly recall, as Mary McGlynn (forthcoming, 2) has noted, 'the hasty enforced movement to Glasgow's perimeter [of the poor and working classes] following the second world war'. More generally, the dangerous homes of *Trick* represent working-class women in the double bind of economic dependence on and emotional attachment to men. Joy is a woman caught between homes: the borders and margins she inhabits point to 'an ambiguity identified with the position of women in society' (Norquay 2000, 67). Further, Galloway shows particular concern for the insignificance of working-class women's place in a society that does not value them. Woman's unresolved place in this new configuration—and in the new gothic novel—is highlighted in the novel: Joy must walk with dread between one home and another.

Galloway does not confine her exploration of the periphery to the plot. In fact, she explores these margins even more aggressively in the novel's typography. *Trick* features thoughts that bleed into the margins of the page, lists, and sentences that trail off. Additionally, Galloway frequently leaves large gaps between paragraphs, seemingly at random, separates sections with three 'o's (ooo), and leaves some pages unnumbered. Text that does not obey the margins is another 'home' in the novel: it is a place for Galloway to explore working-class women's place in and around this home.

The writing in the margins, presumably Joy's subconscious or unvoiced thoughts, appears when Joy is confronted with an emotionally harrowing situation. Thus when Tony, her boss at the betting office, rapes her, the marginal thoughts become more frequent:

> A spark of terrible anger that he could dare say things like this, expecting me to listen. A spark. I swallowed hard and said nothing. I made excuses. Maybe he thought women liked to hear this kind of thing.
>
> warnings s
> when the v
> happens
>
> I didn't pull back when he put his tongue in my mouth, stroked the nipples under the cloth. I gave in….He couldn't find a way inside my dress. I undid the buttons myself to make it quicker.
>
> worst hap
> we can onl
> blame
>
> Is this what you want? I said. Will this keep you happy. He kissed me deeper and wouldn't answer… He whispered, Tell me you like it when I come.
>
> blame ours
>
> Afterwards, he said he wished I had talked more (Galloway 1991b, 175).

Whereas before Joy was trapped in her home by emotional paralysis and lack of resources to go elsewhere, she is now trapped by brute force. Galloway allows Joy an escape route in the text's margins: the reader is privy to her inner thoughts, and the results are disturbing. Hardly the feminist ideal suggested by such departure from standard textual structure, the thoughts in the margins in this case say, 'sometimes there is a presentiment that stops us before it is too late, but often we ignore the warnings so when the worst thing happens we can only blame ourselves.' Like many of Muriel Spark's short novels, where the reader is often unaware of the protagonists' fates until the very end, Joy's blaming of herself does not become clear until the fragments of her thoughts are pieced back together. Here the text in the margins reaffirms Joy's perception that she is complicit in the rape: not only does she 'give in,' refuse to 'pull back,' and undo 'the buttons myself to make it quicker' (147), but she also internalises the notion that the rape is her fault. By exiling Joy's inner feelings to the edge of the page, Galloway further illustrates how women, and women's problems, are forced to dwell in a place of lesser importance. As with Joy's fear of the institution and council house, her body, too, is a false refuge. Here Galloway reinforces the gothic notion of the imperilled heroine, but blurs the line of victim by presenting a victim who blames herself. Though Joy is clearly still a victim, the circumstances under which she was violated take on a painful complexity that Galloway refuses to portray melodramatically.

Joy's sense of unworthiness is more than just an issue of gender marginality: Tony is her boss, but she has acquiesced to his aggressive advances, joining him for dinner and engaging in sexual activity with him, though (until the rape) not intercourse. The boundaries between Tony and Joy's work and personal relationships blur when Tony uses his power as her boss to corner her in the office at work, after the rape:

'He tells me to come with him for cash slips… I have to go. In the back room, he …tries to push me against the wall… Still too skinny, he says… I'm brisk till pay time then run. Outside, I feel the note in my hand and look down, An extra fiver' (205–6).

Joy must obey Tony's orders on the job and finds it less frightening to succumb to his attack than fight him off. Though this is a painfully gendered position, class plays a crucial part as well. Joy's teaching salary is insufficient for her to pay her rent, and even with two jobs she cannot afford the car she so desperately needs to commute to work, and Tony makes it clear he is willing to pay her extra for sexual favours. By contrast, Joy's friend Marianne seems more solvent on the same teaching salary. Marianne lives with her middle-class mother; Joy comes from an impoverished (and dysfunctional) family background that does not provide her with a safety net. A chasm in cultural capital and an implied gulf in understanding colours Joy's relationship with Tony. According to Pamela Fox, 'conventional markers of femininity and masculinity become particularly coveted, as well as scorned… in response to the instability of gender codes in working-class culture' (24), as is the case when Tony courts Joy in the months leading up to her rape. That Tony mistakes Joy's feeble resistance for pleasure during the rape is an outgrowth of these shaky power roles.

The unspeakable

The unspeakable takes many forms in *Trick:* the reader is never informed of Joy's class status, though ample clues are given; Joy is never referred to as Michael's mistress, nor is the term adultery uttered; and Joy vomits any food she eats—more often she does not eat at all—yet she is never called anorexic/bulimic. In part, these unnameable states can be explained by the shame Joy is forced to feel for each of them, but Galloway also shows Joy to be protective over the messily defined bits of her life. Non-naming erases identity, and creates a broader solidarity with women suffering the same fates. For example, the 'non-naming of Glasgow parallels Joy's inability to speak directly of Michael's death or ever actually to use the words *anorexia* or *bulimia* at the same time as it connects her to such places as Dublin, Manchester, and the Bronx' (McGlynn 2001, 18). In short, Joy's non-naming becomes an act of resistance to being boxed in at the same time that it is a result of shame about the state of her life. The unspeakable in gothic literature most often presents itself in metonymic figures: monsters standing in for societal ills, and stormy winds revealing unspoken passions. Joy's anorexia is emblematic of ambivalence about survival: on the one hand, she seeks help and advice from numerous sources, on the other she chooses to waste away.

Trick features magazine advice that serves as a guide to the 'lost' heroine's interior state, and as a 'deconstructive text with a specific agenda in exposing and undermining the language, textual practices, and discourses we live by' (Norquay 2000, 131). McGlynn (2001, 22) correctly points out that 'the short-term, the surface answers offered by magazines only exacerbate [Joy's] distance from the (supposed) concerns of everyday life for most women', and that the magazine 'samples' indicate the hegemonic threat of popular culture, but Joy's relationship to these magazines is more conflicted than McGlynn suggests. Galloway, well aware of the damaging impact of these magazines on women, depicts Joy as both alienated from and moved by the magazines she reads. During one of her lonely nights at home Joy proclaims, 'Tonight I know what to do. I have a new magazine' (Galloway 1991b, 26). A list of articles follows, about fast meals, diets, and how to present oneself and one's home attractively, all geared toward the working female consumer. Finally, Joy reads an advice column. Each of the letters to the columnist, reproduced in the text, breaks off before it is finished; only a few lines are visible of the last one:

> Dear Kathy,
> My husband and I split up about two years ago. I have rebuilt
> my life fairly successfully in most respects but one. I miss

> Blisters. Little moon craters on the smooth paper. I push the magazine
> aside and let the tears drip onto the rug… (28)

Joy reacts to the advice column that reflects too closely her own life's troubles by crying, yet she at first describes the tears as 'blisters.' In fact, this description of Joy's tears implies danger. March (2003, 123) comments that Galloway's heroines 'overflow body boundaries, becoming dangerous both socially and textually'. Joy's 'blisters' burn right into the magazine, and presumably into the page we read. Far from feeling distanced from the '(supposed) concerns of everyday life for most women' (McGlynn 2001, 22), Joy is deeply affected by the similarity between the letter writer's life and her own. However, because of her depression and isolation, Joy is unable to finish reading the letter. She feels alienated only by the lack of real answers the magazine provides.

As Galloway is well aware, women's magazines do enforce a code of femininity on women, particularly damaging to women without sufficient means to implement the magazines' suggestions. The magazines are filled with 'tricks' for women to make their cheap things look more expensive and promise sure-fire answers to all their problems: 'No-nonsense looks for the Working Mum,' and '7 Meals that Make in Minutes,' for example (Galloway 1991b, 39; 26). But Galloway also provides Joy with magazine headlines all her own, such as when Joy writes to herself, 'This is the Way Things Are' (26), betraying her acceptance that she cannot change the way she feels with any number of magazine advice columns. Joy ultimately learns the only 'trick' that the magazines could not teach her: to keep breathing.

Vile bodies

The formal elements of *Trick* often mirror the messages in the plot: 'Like a bulimic, the text regurgitates what it cannot digest, often social messages in conflict with one another that Joy is unable to process' (McGlynn 2001, 17). Stein (1983, 126) reads 'Female Gothic' madness and monsters as instructive critiques of society. Joy's anorexia is monstrous and symbolizes her struggle for autonomy; it is the one thing she has control over. According to McGlynn (*loc. cit.*), 'On the one hand, an anorexic woman reveals an impulse to conform to external societal expectations of feminine appearance, but on the other, she resists reproductive stereotypes, refusing to menstruate and demonstrate her womanhood, actively choosing anorexia as an effective yet dangerous means of asserting an identity'. The regurgitated text is another form of resistance in the novel as well: a refusal to be a consumer. As with the magazine advice that she cannot heed, Joy denies the unjust world she lives in by refusing to participate mentally or physically.

Joy's body and thoughts are never her own. When she writes Marianne a letter Joy claims, 'I am looking over my own shoulder, watching the pen in my hand writing monstrous' (Galloway 1991b, 189). The sentence ends without a period, and is on a page which follows a page blank but for the word 'oops'— off-centre in the middle of the page—reinforcing the lack of control Joy feels when she is in the mental hospital. In one of her memories of Michael's drowning, Joy has an uncontrollable urge to smile, and the *'low hum of voices makes the smile wider. I am not in control of my face'* (39, emphasis in original). Additionally, Galloway frequently portrays Joy's body as fragmented, often brutally so. When Joy takes a bath, she positions the mirror so she can only see her torso and remarks, 'the mirror cuts off my head' (46), and when she takes a photograph in the mirror to send to Marianne, 'The camera bludgeons off half my face and the flash whites out the rest' (156). Joy's corporeal representations cannot truly represent her, they can only illustrate the violent acts she undergoes. Joy refuses to look at her physical body as a unified whole. The disjointed, fragmentary body Joy presents, with its gothic severity, evades her shame and allows her to avoid confronting the pain of Michael's death, as well as the other tragedies in her life.

Galloway's physical description of mothers in *Trick* is subtly menacing. One of Joy's magazines features a story on 'THE BEST MUM IN BRITAIN…who fostered fifteen problem children in the past two years,' a woman who is described by Joy as 'a huge woman with arms like white puddings hanging on butchers' hooks' (163), hardly an appetizing image for a woman averse to eating. Similarly, Joy sees Marianne's mother Ellen, who serves as a surrogate mother for Joy when Marianne leaves for the United States, as dangerous because her effort at mothering is to feed Joy, anathema to Joy's anorexia. Of the novel's surrogate/adoptive mothers—Ellen, the health visitor, the 'best mum,' and Myra—only Myra is not portrayed as either overweight or obsessed with food, though even she seems larger than life. Ellen constantly tries to feed Joy, the health visitor is portrayed as more eager to eat Joy's cookies than to make sure she is healthy, and the mother featured in the magazine is explicitly perceived by Joy as a piece of meat. Unlike Joy, these women are consumers, both of food and perhaps by extension everything else that Joy has forsaken in her grief. Galloway presents these women as both physically healthier and more gluttonous than Joy, thereby expressing ambivalence about the politics of consumption. Like Joy's anorexic/bulimic body, these women's bodies are depicted as monstrous, but they are disturbing to the status quo for different reasons: they threaten to consume too much instead of too little, challenging the established order.

Further emphasizing the ambivalence toward family, the hospital residents prove a poor family substitute. When Joy goes for dinner with her fellow patients, she is painfully, yet subtly, reminded of Michael when two of the patients go off for a kiss and there is a smell of chlorine reminiscent of Michael's drowning in a pool. Though Galloway does not explicitly mention Michael, Joy responds to the stimuli: 'The hollow echo and the smell of chlorine makes my head sore. But this is what there is now. I sit at the table with people I don't know and try to love them more. We are sharing the terrible minutes together. There must be something touching in that… John leaves the table fast, clipping my elbow. He's going to be sick' (169). The only thing Joy can share with this adopted family, as with her own sister, is a penchant for overdrinking, binging and purging. As with Joy's surrogate mothers and her own anorexic/bulimic urges, the inmates of the institution express various degrees of ambivalence about the world through their eating and drinking rituals, and serve as monstrous reminders of the culture that hides them away. Dismissed as 'mad,' these highly emotional people reflect badly on a culture that values productivity over health.

Throughout the novel Joy mimics normative middle-class behaviour: she cleans the house for Mr Dick; makes tea for two with one teabag and 'take[s] it through as though I've really made it in a pot and just poured it out' for the health visitor (20); lives in a cottage that looks more costly than it is; and imitates bourgeois marriage with both Paul and Michael. But each of these efforts to appear middle class is undermined by Joy's class position. As a working-class woman in a society that values the appearance of affluence, sanity, and health, but is less concerned with how these are obtained, it is little wonder Joy has a breakdown. Galloway shrewdly challenges this value system by appropriating the gothic genre and using it to point out that endangered homes and monstrous bodies are indicative of more than just psychological disturbance. By illuminating the economic and social conditions of Joy's life, Galloway pushes gothic fiction in a new direction.

Works cited

Bissett, Alan (Ed) (2001) *Damage Land: New Scottish Gothic Fiction.* Edinburgh: Polygon.

Ellis, Kate Ferguson (1989) *The Contested Castle: Gothic Novels and the Subversion of Domestic Ideology.* Urbana and Chicago: U Illinois P.

Fox, Pamela (1994) *Class Fictions: Shame and Resistance in the British Working-Class Novel, 1890–1945.* Durham, NC: Duke UP.

Galloway, Janice (1995) *Foreign Parts.* Normal, Ilinois: Dalkey Archive Press.

—— (1991) 'Frostbite.' *Blood.* New York: Random House.

—— (1991) *The Trick is to Keep Breathing.* London: Minerva [1989].

March, Cristie L. (2003) *Rewriting Scotland: Welsh, Warner, Banks, Galloway and Kennedy.* Manchester: Manchester UP.

Massé, Michelle (1992) *In the Name Love: Women, Masochism, and the Gothic.* Ithaca and London: Cornell UP.

McGlynn, Mary (2001) 'Janice Galloway.' *Review of Contemporary Fiction* 21:2, 7–41.

—— (forthcoming) 'Janice Galloway's Alienated Spaces.' *Scottish Studies Review.*

McGrath, Patrick and Bradford Morrow (Eds.) (1991) *The New Gothic.* New York: Random House.

Norquay, Glenda (2000) 'Janice Galloway's Fraudulent Mooching.' *Contemporary Scottish Women Writers.* Christianson, Aileen and Alison Lumsden (eds). Edinburgh: Edinburgh UP. 131–43.

Punter, David (1996) *The Literature of Terror: A History of Gothic Fictions 1765 to the Present Day, Volume 2: The Modern Gothic.* New York: Addison Wesley Longman.

—— (1999) 'Heart Lands: Contemporary Scottish Gothic.' *Gothic Studies* 1:1, 101–18.

Stein, Karen F. (1983) 'Monsters and Madwomen: Changing Female Gothic.' *The Female Gothic.* Juliann E. Fleenor (ed). Montreal and London: Eden Press, 123–37.

Writing the flow

Adam Piette

Boy Book See

Janice Galloway. Glasgow: Mariscat Press, 2002

One of the strange things about cryptosporidium (apart from its ability to trigger scary war between Mugdock nimbies and water-drinking folk in Glasgow) is that it wants to kill its hosts through dehydration. So the parasite causes diarrhoea, weight loss and abdominal cramping because it's *thirsty*. Maybe the Drinking Water Quality Regulator and Scottish Water should take note. One way they could do this is to read Janice Galloway's new book of poetry, *Boy Book See*, which has a whole section on water, at the heart of which is the hard word 'cryptosporidium'. It occurs in a witty improvisation on whisky, 'scotch', which redefines *uisge beatha* as modern water, including the waters flowing from Mugdock. Water, and not the water of life, is repackaged and rebranded in Galloway's fantasy as a new medicine, AQUA-HYDRO-VITE®:

> the active ingredient is hydrogenated oxygen (raw) infused with any or all
> of chlorine, lead, aluminium, iron and manganese fluoride,
> cryptosporidium, pesticides, disinfection byproducts (soluble and
> insoluble) and Blue-Green Algae. The most noticeable and attractive of
> these ingredients is Blue-Green Algae.

Galloway turns eco-Green at the thought of the controlled contamination of the essential element. 'Water and freedom gang thegither', the collection argues.

A good reader is as thirsty for words as cryptosporidium is for our inner waters, and that may have something to do with how we feel about literary language. We say we like clear, transparent, flowing words, as if texts were clean rivers come to slake our need for fiction and artifice. Galloway's writing in *Book Boy See* resists such easy thirsts, opting for a choppy, dense and difficult verbal texture that forces us to stop and think rather than comfortably drink. The collection is written in a variety of styles, satirical parody, childhood memoir, experimental poetry, prose fantasy, love letter, one-liners. It is a prosy collection nevertheless, much of the best writing taking the form of prose-poetic meditations. These avoid the garrulousness of big projects like *Clara*, and zero in on concentrated topics with power and panache. As with all good collections, we are invited to meditate on the secret lines of force and the energy-flows that connect the pieces. The water section works alongside a series of poems about childhood and we can begin to intuit connections: both water and childhood stimulate surmise about origins, about elemental experiences and their shaping power, about the growth of the imagination and its early life in the flow of experience, flow of words. And, for Galloway, both topics meet in ecology, since our concern about the water we drink is inflected by fear about the future of life on earth, the future as imagined in our children.

The collection opens with a charming and intimate poem, 'boy book see', about a mother's vigilance over her son as she battles to keep the house clean of a potentially polluted environment:

> all day feels like
> wiping down a constant
> cloth or suede a snail-trail in the hand
> bacteria a thousand swarms diseases viral spores this
> vigilance is
> never quite enough

The lines acknowledge the freaky dirt-paranoia of parenting at the same time as forcing us, through the disintegrating shock of the line-breaks, to feel the weary burden of those fears too. And we are asked to feel them beyond the confines of the domestic space. The son is pictured reaching for a blue book from a shelf, and it is an atlas, representing 'all the world/its seas'. A mother's deep anxieties about the cleanliness of the environment expand to include the whole world, out to the seas, source of the aqua-hydro-vite so vital to the future. What we might too easily dismiss as a mother's unreasonable neurosis becomes a larger and troubling ecological concern, which we must all share (for 'we all are water', as Lennon sang).

The way you bring up a child recalls the ways you were brought up. This is something of a pointless commonplace until you read Galloway. The poem about the mother is full of tiny domestic detail, as though each thing in the house were at once comfortingly familiar and strangely menacing, perhaps harbouring the invisible bacteria of uncontrollable forces. The kitchen is 'thick with pine and peaches/washing peelings tea and rags', we are told. These are homely details, homeliness as the source of all that is maternal-sentimental, one might have thought. But the details can become neurotic fetishes if they become hiding-places for those viral spores (homeliness, like godliness, being next to cleanliness), as the next line implies: 'the antiseptic in your hand a brimful bottles/(cot death meningitis measles horseflies dark decay)'. When Galloway writes about her own childhood in the longest and strongest piece in the collection, 'this much is constant', we are treated to a similar catalogue of details, as though sharpened and defined by the lens of fearful memory.

Memory seems to be interrogating the recalled images, as though a difficult question were being asked, something about the relations between the words 'home', 'childhood', 'fear' and 'determination', something about the ways the act of seeing those things so clearly then may have been charged with the menace of being seen: being seen by the monitory gaze of the parent, or even being seen by the objects themselves. For the child is in her mother's bedroom, transgressing the site with her sight:

A fire vent over the bedstead, its handle, waiting open. It glints like teeth in the dark, makes a sound like sore bones. You don't want to get closer but it is coming anyway, sidling up. Without wanting to, you lift your eyes to the s-shaped slits. Draw your eye to the beautiful moulded rims. Look. Careful of dust, blown-back soot, the smell of burning.

The monstrous object, as the librettist of *Monster* knows, is a mother's mouth, an *it* that seeks to gobble the child up. The mother is uncanny, a thing from below, a creature of destruction and fire like a dragon: the homely is turned into the monstrous by a child's fearful reckoning: 'Mother is under the floorboards. That noise is her, moving about cleaning something.' Real Mother is downstairs, cleaning, the words say. But they also say, Monstrous Mother is dead, underground, Death obsessively controlling the things in the house, watching me secretly watching her things through the dark eyes of the fire vent. And it is the same control exercised by the mother in 'boy book see', control as the contagious neurosis of cleanliness. The girl's imagination begins, the story tells us, in an act of transgression, entering the private zone of the double mother daring to see as she sees, to see the things she privately sees, imagining as looking through the s-shaped slits of the death-mother's eyes. And what makes this so menacing is the terrible internalisation of monitory code, of the mother's fear of virus, dirt, bacteria transformed by deep culture into a technology of fear and death: 'Careful of dust, blown-back soot, the smell of burning.'

Boy Book See is tremendously closely-written, seeing through the s-shaped slits of culture's obsessiveness about generation and protectiveness, through to its roots in a gendered set of forces that have served to demonise the woman in the domestic sphere. The work on mothers here links out to the concerns with the global environment by exploring the hinterland of ideology, the ideology of restrictive forms and walls which have boxed women into the role of parenting the future consumers of the world. A network of forces caused generations of women to clean flats and houses neurotically, worry themselves to distraction over the health of their children. These neuroses and anxieties are internalised by children to create the monster of culture, the mother under the floorboards, secretly watching from a dark and fiery purgatorial realm. It is the *same* network, Galloway argues, that controls our water supply—and yet we are seduced into blaming our mothers by the ways we see the world.

'Mons Meg: *A fluid fairytale*' (almost) closes the collection and is a medieval fantasy about the construction of Mugdock reservoir, with Glasgow as 'Castlegate'. It is comic, imaginative and beautifully told. Meg is a woman sacrificed to preserve the reservoir and its community from harm: 'they killed the smallest and most pious of the women and settled her body into the simmering lime-slurry at the bottom of the pit, a peewit feather in her bluing hand'. The peewit is the lapwing, whose cry ('peewit') was said to be the witch's call: 'Bewitched!' It is Meg's death which, psychically and culturally speaking, keeps the waters clear and clean, as in the sacrifice of the community's witch: 'And since, they say, Meg's nourishment kept the waters of the Castlegate fair.'

This is deep writing, nosing out the hidden contamination of culture, the culture of contamination, writing which discovers the secret witch-hunt that distorts honourable ecological concern, bonds between human beings and the ways the imagination sees. Remember Meg and feel real guilt, real anger, lay the blame where it really lies, the writing asks: 'Picture her under the city slabs and engine noise, good citizens.'

Exchanges: *Clara*

Interview with Janice Galloway

Linda Jackson

LINDA JACKSON: Clearly there has been a huge amount of research done in the writing of Clara. Can you tell me something about that research process?

JANICE GALLOWAY: The research was not only huge it was sprawlingly, almost uncontainably and possibly even unnecessarily huge. This partly from my natural preference to stand on as much STUFF as possible before I start, and from the range of things I wanted to know. There's obvious research (names, dates, figures) then the unobvious stuff (likely patterns of wallpaper, preferences in teaching methods of under-fives, fashions for women's walking boots etc.), which is certainly as crucial to the process of constructing what is meant, once it's finished, to read as a living consciousness.

I started with the Schumanns themselves and in their own words— volumes of letters and diaries and journals and lord knows what else to each other, friends and acquaintances like Brahms and Verhulst and Viardot, and to their families. There were household books, notes and jottings with which I could get an idea of the running of the household and how they spend their money, also what they did when they were running out (which they frequently did). Alongside that I could use medical reports and autopsy papers, love-letters and pictures of the children—anything that might give a texture to their personalities and everyday environment. What mattered—what matters in general to my writing—was that everydayness, that mundanity and detail. I knew from the first I did not want to write about 'genius', for want of a better term, as a separate state. What makes people interesting to me is not what the world later decides is their 'achievement' so much as the circumstances under which their lives were lived and their work produced *merely as their everyday work*. Which, of course, is what it was. To root the whole thing in practical reality, and quite doggedly, almost, get away from academic or elitist notions of artists being 'different people' was part of the point, so there had to be a great deal of detail—the texture of a life rests in the detail. Aside from that, of course, I also read a political and military history of middle-Europe, books on clothes and household management, transport, obstetrics and medical material in general, especially the care of the mentally disturbed—anything that could add to my idea of what their everyday realities might have been. I read the books they enjoyed, and the books they thought they ought to read, which were often different. I read Robert Schumann's own literary and musical criticism and Clara's transcription notes and, of course, read and listened to a lot of music: musicians, both players and composers, say a good deal about themselves in non-verbal ways.

This lot, of course, sat on top of the biographies—both of the Schumanns and Mendelssohn, Brahms, Paganini, Liszt etc.—for chronology. Chronology is not important *in itself*, but matters as clay. The better the grip you have on that clay, the more convincingly, or organically, maybe, the final work can be shaped. The work, however, its shape and pace, matter more than the clay itself. Of the bios, Berthold Litzmann's three-volume work on Clara was certainly the one I used most often. What helped root the whole thing once all that reading was well under way (it was never *finished*, how could it be *finished*?) was visiting places that had been meaningful to either Clara or Robert as individuals. Looking into the Rhine from the bridge in Düsseldorf not far from Bilkerstrasse, where they lived when Robert attempted suicide, or visiting the Thomas Kirche in Leipzig, for example, was very powerful. The real motivator, however, for any work of fiction has to be in the white space: most people do not lucidly articulate their lives, or shy away from revealing, even to themselves, what is too close to the bone. The gaps in the diaries, contradictions between his and her accounts of things, the unspoken, unrecorded trenches of childhood were where I saw my way in. The background research, its facts and pack-drills were a room to work inside: the empathetic reconstructing of a credible psychology from those facts—that's

166

the work. To allude to motivation and deeper character, the hows and whys and tangential nature of decisions and things that change a life is the novel's territory. But the writing of any book, research or no, is accomplished in the same way, which means alone, with as much tactile imagination as is musterable. The research is almost neither here nor there to that process.

What inspired you to research and write about Clara Schumann?

The truth is you don't really know what attracts you to something at the time, and though I can certainly offer rationales now, I'm not sure they'd be that interesting or illuminating. I suppose I've always been motivated by trying to express silence or silent states of being, silent people, or people who are constrained from telling their own story for one reason or another. Or who say it and no one listens. I'm interested in what silences people, what frees people from silence—and indeed how many lies can be told by those who 'speak out', either because they are not aware of 'other truths' or simply through lack of self-knowledge. I'm interested very much in watchers, and in women and children and servants and seamstresses and the last desk player right at the back of the second-violins—the generally unrecorded voices in all sorts of histories. Clara's story is full of resonances that would appeal to me on that score alone. Added to that, I've always been interested in what music is and is not (and what musicians and their work is and is not); what Art might be and who serves it and how; what appears to be the case and what actually is the case; what history records and what it ignores or relegates as 'unimportant', and complex psychological dilemmas—which suggests Clara Schumann as a more or less tailor-made subject. The spur came from listening to (and loving) Robert Schumann's *Frauenliebe und Leben* (*A Woman's Life and Love*), and wondering how to place the real woman in Robert's life at the centre of things instead of this fantasy woman invented by Robert and his chosen poet, Chamisso, in the song cycle. The book has eight chapters to mirror the eight songs, but allowing the titles to mean very different things. It was also important that this book was for a general reader—it's not a music book, not a biography for a specialist. It's a story about a woman trying to cope with near-incompatible ideals, trying to maintain her own moral imperatives. My greatest respect is for the general reader, who is simply enthused by the human condition and its contradictions.

How does the structure of the book relate to the Schumann song cycle?

The eight-song structure of the cycle was already in place for me to use. I was attracted to it since it's extraordinarily beautiful, but it's also hard to cope with in a modern context. That the woman in the cycle sings that her life begins when she first sees the man she loves, for example; that her only yearning is to be married and to give birth to a baby who resembles her husband is, to put it mildly, questionable to the modern mind-set. It wasn't hard to wonder how different the real 'life and love' of Clara Schumann had been to this naïve, and wholly male-constructed portrait. In structural terms, simply placing my female-constructed recreation of a real woman's life against the titles of each of the songs would accomplish its own commentary—it was that stark. There is no earthly reason, however, why anyone would need to know the songs to read the book. There's no demand being made—the titling of the chapters to make it accessible to those who wanted to clue in if they wanted to.

The sections of the book that describe Robert's manic episodes must have been very difficult to gauge. What challenges did writing these states throw up for you?

None but the usual challenges, really—how do you write someone so they emerge as credible, visceral on the page? Imagining a character like that depends a great deal on a kind of acting: the imagining of the character hinges for me upon acting my way into the part, then writing it from inside as much as I can. There was certainly a self-imposed demand that Robert should be credible and never 'cartoon' nuts. I hate the flaccid idea of 'genius' being akin to 'madness', where neither term is taken seriously or evaluated with much empathy or practical insight. That geniuses—whoever they might be—are merely us, that so-called Great Work and Great Men (almost invariably Men) are indeed merely Other People who have a lot in common with ourselves seems very difficult for the elitist mentality to grasp. That 'madmen' work from rationales of their own making likewise. I also abhor the more modern tendency to romanticise mental illness as a form of creativity or, worse, as mere 'stress'. Psychotic illness is certainly suffering for the individual experiencing the breakdown, and often for the family around them. Robert's illness, from my reading of his own notes, from his hospital records and in his own estimation was certainly horrible and certainly illness and I wished to show it as such, with its attendant pain as well as its inner workings. Mania attempts to rationalize itself—and to catch ordinary rationalisation on the hop to 'prove' itself superior. Genuine madness does not merely rave, and neither is it 'creative' in any meaningful sense: it often acts with an alarming consistency, in the way physical illness does, to an expected pattern. Even so, writing Robert was easy compared to writing Clara: unusual psychologies and extremes of behaviour are MUCH easier to write than enforced calm.

There seem to be extended metaphors of silence and distancing in your representation of Clara. Was it difficult to render the character in this way?

Pretty much as above. As with the women in *Foreign Parts* who are reluctant to be emotionally open with each other and who don't speak the language of the country they are travelling through, Clara, as a character who absented herself from her surroundings in order to view and gain some kind of control, was more difficult to write than more volatile characters. The demand was to find other, consistent ways to suggest the hidden or concealed emotional response beneath. Since a priority with writing this book was to re-negotiate a female space inside an otherwise very masculine tale—Clara could very easily be seen as the adjunct of first her father, then her husband, a woman without a mother or female friends or even other female artists in her life, a woman whose female help with her domestic circumstances are seen as 'irrelevant'— writing this through the silence that was often expected or demanded of Clara was imperative. Rendering a still, self-contained, yet deeply passionate person whilst making that stillness gripping, making it the central focus, is the toughest thing I've done. I think. Writing good girls, as opposed to bad, sad, mad or raving girls or boys, is tough. We're so trained—movies, telly, music and stories—into enthusiasm for the feckless, the reckless, the riotous or the extreme. Writing Liszt was falling off a log by comparison with writing Clara, the moral imperative of Clara's very quiet, very unfashionable heroism. That was the frightening thing—that Clara had no access to or enthusiasm for irony, snide asides, smart put-downs. I had to 'vulnerablise' the twenty-first century voice I was more used to writing in and be prepared to open the character up in what was, for me at least, a more terrifyingly direct way.

Can you say why you have ended the telling of Clara's life at the death of Robert? Can you envisage writing some other piece on the remaining part of her life?

The song-cycle ends with the man's death and a suggestion (in the song cycle it is embedded in the piano part alone) of the woman's continuance. Also, more pressingly, perhaps, the book was already some four hundred and twenty pages by that stage—to write another forty years of Clara's life on top would have resulted in a stupidly long and rather indigestible pudding, even if I had wanted to. It was nothing but relief to finish the book after six years and no, I can't EVER imagine writing her again, or doing the subsequent forty-year widowhood. Dear god no. The thought of all that editing alone brings me out in a rash.

Monster *and then* Clara. *How important is music as inspiration for you as a writer?*

Very. I studied music with a fine man called Ken Hetherington when I was in my senior secondary school years, and again at University, though the real 'study' part, and the one-to-one attention to make it particularly fulfilling, was with Ken. I had no thought but to become other than a musician or musicologist of some kind until I reached university and found that a good deal of it was lonely, mathematical, sometimes pedantic and, in the physical as well as mental demands of playing, extraordinarily circular. That takes a very particular temperament, that kind of graft for that kind of reward: what that temperament might be is tracked a little in the novel. It's certainly not mine. But being a musician, especially a performer, is a very resonant thing for me, a great metaphor for concealment, survival and struggle. Then again, the music of language, of how the words bounce and resonate as sentences, lists, broken lines—that has always been very important indeed to me. If I can't HEAR the words as they go onto the page, I can't seem to keep writing them down. I lose them. This is true especially of 'voices' of characters—I need to be able to hear a beat or metre in each voice to be convinced what I'm writing is working. In stories where no voice is dominant, or where no characters appear (I do have some!) the bounce and rhythm of the words becomes even more important. I wouldn't divide that enthusiasm and motivation from prose, though there's a lot of suggestion it's 'poetic'. Not with me. That's how prose works for me.

I like working with musicians. It's not only the chance to re-involve with a former life, so to speak, it's the chance to use the head in collaboration and in a slightly different way, where words don't control outcomes to the same extent. That kind of control over end-product with novels is a powerful responsibility, but also powerfully aesthetically satisfying. Collaborating with musicians or artists is satisfying in a wholly different way—having the company and the other ideas to add to your own necessarily breaches boundaries and shifts ground. If it doesn't, it's not really doing its job.

Just listening to music on CDs though, that's always been a take-or-leave with me. Too passive. The fun of the music is the same as the fun of constructing words into a story or a novel. I need to feel involved, invited, able to alter the shapes. Part of the thing. Otherwise, why bother?

Notes on Contributors

Colin Clark is a writer and a teacher. He lives in Glasgow and is a graduate of the Creative Writing M.Phil at Glasgow University.

Ailsa Crum lives in Glasgow and is writing her first novel.

Josianne Paccaud-Huguet is Professor of English at l'Université Lumière, Lyons.

Ellen-Raïssa Jackson works for the BBC and lives in Edinburgh.

Linda Jackson is a Nietzsche scholar who lectures in English and Media in Glasgow; she has three children and also enjoys writing and working as a musician.

Eve Lazovitz works at the University of Dartmouth, Maine.

Alexis Logsdon will commence a PhD on finishing her bachelor's degree.

Willy Maley is Professor of Renaissance Studies at the University of Glasgow. His publications include *Salvaging Spenser: Colonialism, Culture and Identity* and *Nation State and Empire: Shakespeare to Milton*.

Carolyn Masel lives and works in Melbourne, where she teaches American literature. She is a published poet and has three children.

Sharon Norris is a freelance writer and teacher. She works for the Open University.

Darragh O'Grady lives and works in Mexico. He holds an MA in English on the novels of Janice Galloway and Irvine Welsh.

Adam Piette is Reader in English Literature at Glasgow University and is the author of *Remembering the Sound of Words* and *Imagination at War: a reader*.

Subscribe to Edinburgh Review

Individual subscriptions (3 issues annually) £17 / $27 / €27
Institutional subscriptions (3 issues annually) £34 / $54 / €54

Please complete and return this subscription form to Edinburgh Review, 22a, Buccleuch Place, Edinburgh, EH8 9LN

BACK ISSUES are available at £5. Please contact our office for availability information or to place an order.

Subscription Form

Name: _____

Address: _____

_____

_____

Postcode: _____

I wish to subscribe to the Edinburgh Review, beginning from issue _____ .

I enclose payment for £17 (individual) / £34 (institutional) *

[* = delete as applicable]

Please make cheques payable to 'Edinburgh Review'

To pay by Credit / Debit Card, please complete details below:

Type of Card : VISA / Mastercard / Switch [Delete as appropriate]

Card Number : _____ _____ _____ _____

Card Valid from : __ / __ / __ to : __ / __ / __ Issue No : __ [Switch only]

Signature : _____ Date : __ / __ / __